What is a map?

These small maps explain the meaning of some of the lines and colours on the atlas maps.

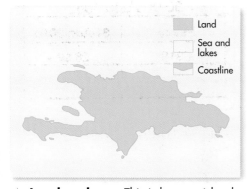

Land and sea This is how an island [sh]own on a map. The land is coloured [green] and the sea is blue. The coastline [is] a line.

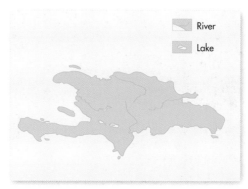

2. Rivers and lakes There are some lakes on the island and rivers that flow down to the sea.

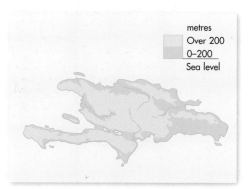

3. Height of the land – 1 This map shows the land over 200 metres high in a lighter colour. The height of the land is shown by contour lines and layer colours.

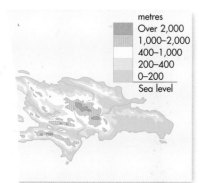

4. H[eigh]t of the land – 2 This map s[how]s more contour lines and layer colours. [It] shows that the highest land is in the centre of the island and that it is over 2,000 metres high.

5. Countries This is a way of showing different information about the island. It shows that the island is divided into two countries. They are separated by a country boundary.

6. Cities and towns There are cities and towns on the island. The two capital cities are shown with a special symbol. Other large or important cities are also shown by a red square or circle.

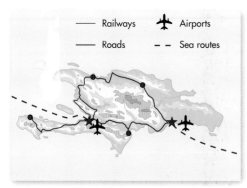

7. Transport information This map shows the most important roads, railways, airports and sea routes. Transport routes connect the cities and towns.

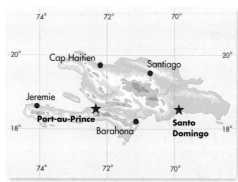

8. Where is the island? This map gives the lines of latitude and longitude and shows where the island is in the world. Page 59 in the atlas shows the same island at a different scale.

9. A complete map – using the country colouring and showing the letter-figure codes used in the index.

Scale

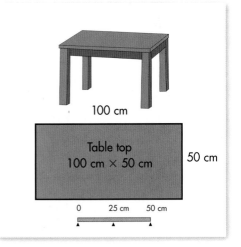

This is a drawing of the top of a table, looking down on it. It is 100 cm wide and 50 cm from front to back. The drawing measures 4 × 2 cm. It is drawn to scale: 1 cm on the drawing equals 25 cm on the table.

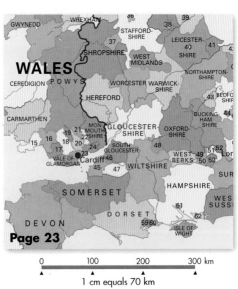

This is a plan of a room looking down from above. 1 cm on the map equals 1 metre in the room. The same table is shown, but now at a smaller scale. Use the scale bar to find the measurements of other parts of the room.

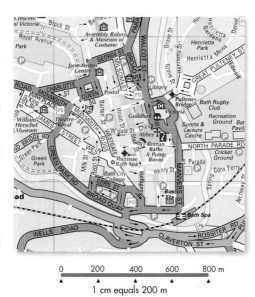

1 cm equals 200 m

This is a map of an area in the city of Bath. Large buildings can be seen but other buildings are too small to show. Below are atlas maps of different scales.

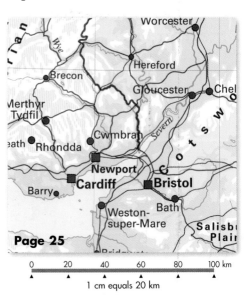

Page 25

0   20   40   60   80   100 km

1 cm equals 20 km

Scale bars

This distance represents 1 mile

This distance represents 1 kilometre

These examples of scale bars are at the scale of 1 cm equals 0.5 km

Page 23

0   100   200   300 km

1 cm equals 70 km

Signposts still have miles on them. 1 mile = 1.6 km, or 10 miles is the same as 16 kilometres. On maps of continents in this atlas, both a kilometre and a mile scale bar are shown.

Page 50

0   300   600 km

1 cm equals 150 km

On the maps of the continents, where you cannot see the British Isles, a small map of the British Isles is shown. It gives you some idea of size and scale.

BRITISH ISLES
On same scale

Direction

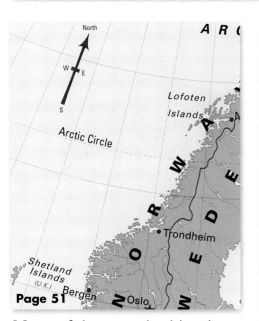

Page 51

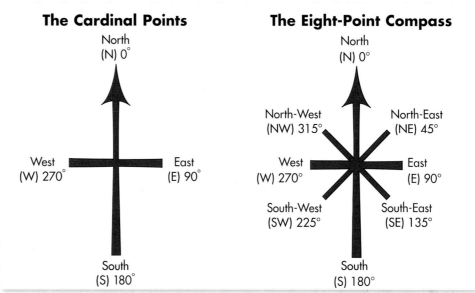

The Cardinal Points

North
(N) 0°

West
(W) 270°

East
(E) 90°

South
(S) 180°

The Eight-Point Compass

North
(N) 0°

North-West
(NW) 315°

North-East
(NE) 45°

West
(W) 270°

East
(E) 90°

South-West
(SW) 225°

South-East
(SE) 135°

South
(S) 180°

Many of the maps in this atlas have a North Point showing the direction of north. It points in the same direction as the lines of longitude. The four main directions shown are called the cardinal points.

Direction is measured in degrees. This diagram shows the degree numbers for each cardinal point. The direction is measured clockwise from north. The diagram on the right shows all the points of the compass and the divisions between the cardinal points. For example, between north and east there is north-east, between south and west is south-west. You can work out the cardinal points at your home by looking for the sun rising in the east and setting in the west.

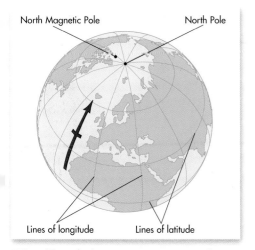

The Earth has a spot near the North Pole that is called the Magnetic Pole. If a piece of metal that was magnetized at one end was left to float, then the magnetized tip would point to the North Magnetic Pole.

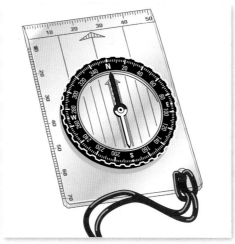

The needle of a compass is magnetized and it always points north. If you know where you are and want to go to another place, you can measure your direction from a map and use a compass to guide you.

Page 25

This is part of map 25. North is at the top. Look at the points of the compass on the diagram above and the positions of places on the map. Taunton is north-east of Exeter and Dorchester is south-east of Taunton.

Latitude and longitude

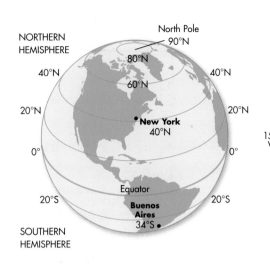

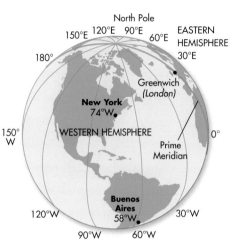

Latitude

This map shows part of the Earth seen from thousands of kilometres above New York. The Equator is exactly halfway between the North and South Poles. It divides the Earth into two hemispheres. The Equator is shown as a line on maps. It is numbered 0°. There are other lines on maps north and south of the Equator. They are called lines of latitude.

Longitude

Maps have another set of lines running north to south linking the Poles. These lines are called lines of longitude. The line numbered 0° runs through Greenwich in London, England, and is called the Prime Meridian. The other lines of longitude are numbered up to 180° east and west of 0°. Longitude line 180° runs through the Pacific Ocean.

Map references

The latitude and longitude lines on maps form a grid. In this atlas, the grid lines are in blue, and on most maps are shown for every ten degrees. The numbers of the lines can be used to give a reference to show the location of a place on a map. The index in this atlas uses another way of finding places. It lists the rows of latitude as numbers and the columns of longitude as letters.

Line of latitude with its number in degrees
Line of longitude with its number in degrees
Row number used in the index
Column letter used in the index

	Latitude	Longitude	Map page	Map letter-figure
Cairo, Africa	30°N	31°E	55	F2
Mexico City, N. America	19°N	99°W	59	H7
Mumbai, Asia	18°N	72°E	53	H7
Moscow, Europe	55°N	37°E	51	Q4
Sao Paulo, S. America	24°S	48°W	61	F6
Sydney, Oceania	34°S	151°E	57	F11

This table shows the largest city in each continent with its latitude and longitude. Look for them on the maps in this atlas.

Map information

Symbols

Page 17

△ A map symbol shows the position of something – for example, circles for towns or an aeroplane for an airport.

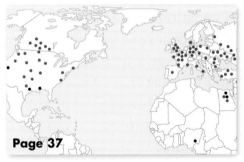
Page 37

△ On some maps a dot or a symbol stands for a large number – for example, ten million people or two million tonnes of wheat or potatoes.

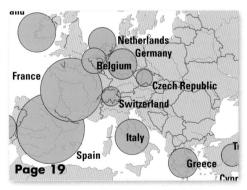
Page 19

△ The size of the symbol can be bigger or smaller, to show different numbers. The symbol here shows tourists.

Colours

Page 51

△ Colours are used on some maps so that separate areas, such as countries, as in this map, can be seen clearly.

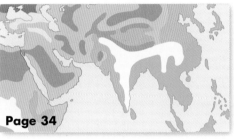
Page 34

△ Patterns on maps often spread across country borders. This map shows different types of vegetation in the world.

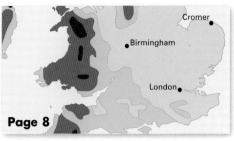
Page 8

△ On other maps, areas that are the same in some way have the same colour to show patterns. This map shows rainfall.

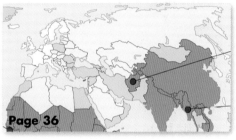
Page 36

△ Colours that are lighter or darker are used on some maps to show less or more of something. This map shows farming.

Graphs and charts

Graphs and charts are used to give more information about subjects shown on the maps. A graph shows how something changes over time.

This graph shows the rainfall for each month in a year as a blue bar that can be measured on the scale at the side of the graph.

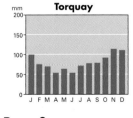
Page 8

This diagram is called a pie-chart. It shows how you can divide a total into its parts.

Page 15

This is a bar-chart. It is another way of showing a total divided into parts.

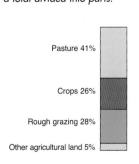

Pasture 41%

Crops 26%

Rough grazing 28%

Other agricultural land 5%

Page 13

Rocks, mountains and rivers

Rocks

This map shows the different types of rock in Great Britain and Ireland.

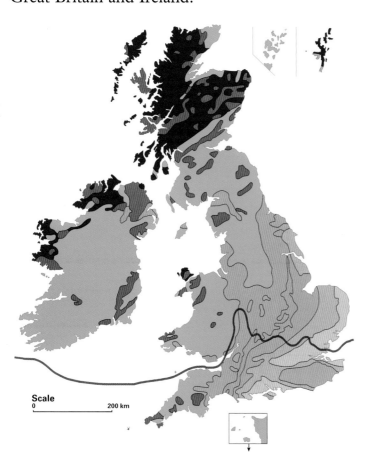

Scale
0 _____ 200 km

Type of rock

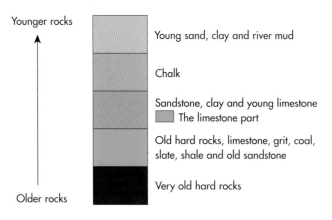

Younger rocks ↑

Young sand, clay and river mud

Chalk

Sandstone, clay and young limestone
The limestone part

Old hard rocks, limestone, grit, coal, slate, shale and old sandstone

Very old hard rocks

Older rocks

Old volcanoes, granite and basalt

Glaciers came as far south as this line up to 10,000 years ago

Longest rivers

(length in kilometres)

Shannon	370
Severn	354
Thames	335
Trent	297
Aire	259
Ouse	230
Wye	215
Tay	188
Nene	161
Clyde	158

Largest islands

(square kilometres)

Great Britain	229,880
Ireland	84,400
Lewis and Harris	2,225
Skye	1,666
Shetland (Mainland)	967
Mull	899
Anglesey	714
Islay	615
Isle of Man	572
Isle of Wight	381

Largest lakes

(square kilometres)

Lough Neagh	382
Lough Corrib	168
Lough Derg	120
Lower Lough Erne	105
Loch Lomond	71
Loch Ness	57

The largest lake in England is Lake Windermere (15 square kilometres). The largest lake in Wales is Lake Vyrnwy (8 square kilometres).

Highest mountains

(height in metres)

In Scotland:
  Ben Nevis 1,347
In Wales:
  Snowdon 1,085
In Ireland:
  Carrauntoohill 1,041
In England:
  Scafell Pike 978
In Northern Ireland:
  Slieve Donard 852

Scale
0 _____ 200 km

Height of the land

metres

- Over 500
- 100–500
- 0–100 — Sea level
- Below sea level

Sea and lakes

North
W — E
S

Shetland Islands

Orkney Islands

Cape Wrath

Pentland Firth

Duncansby Head

Outer Hebrides

Lewis

Harris

Inner Hebrides

Skye

North West Highlands

Moray Firth

Kinnairds Head

Loch Ness

Cairn Gorm ▲ 1245

Ben Nevis ▲ 1347

Grampian Mountains

Mull

Tay

ATLANTIC OCEAN

Loch Lomond

Firth of Forth

Clyde

Islay

Firth of Clyde

Arran

Malin Head

North Channel

Southern Uplands

Tweed

NORTH SEA

Ireland

Donegal Bay

Lower Lough Erne

Lough Neagh

Solway Firth

Tyne

Great Britain

Lake District

Scafell Pike ▲ 978

Lake Windermere

Tees

Mourne Mountains
▲ 852
Slieve Donard

Isle of Man

Pennines

Flamborough Head

Lough Corrib

Lough Ree

IRISH SEA

Aire

Humber

Galway Bay

Shannon

Lough Derg

Barrow

Wicklow Mountains

Liverpool Bay

Anglesey

Snowdon ▲ 1085

Lake Vyrnwy

Trent

The Wash

The Fens

Ouse

Nene

Carrauntoohill ▲ 1041

Blackwater

Saint George's Channel

Cardigan Bay

Cambrian Mountains

Wye

Severn

Avon

Cotswolds

Chiltern Hills

Cape Clear

Bristol Channel

Exmoor

Thames

North Downs

South Downs

Beachy Head

Strait of Dover

France

Dartmoor

Lyme Bay

Isle of Wight

ENGLISH CHANNEL

CELTIC SEA

Land's End

Scilly Isles

France

Channel Islands

Scale

0 — 100 km — 200 km

Weather and climate

Rainfall is measured at many places in the UK every day. Each year, all the measurements are put together and graphs are made, like the ones shown on this page. Experts in the weather use these measurements to find out the average amount of rainfall in the UK for each year. They can then show this on weather maps, like the map below. Graphs and maps are also made for average temperatures and other types of weather (see opposite page). These help the experts to see patterns in the UK's weather over a long period of time. These patterns in the weather show a country's climate. The maps on these pages show you the climate of Great Britain and Ireland.

If you collect the rainfall each day and measure it, then you could draw a graph like this.

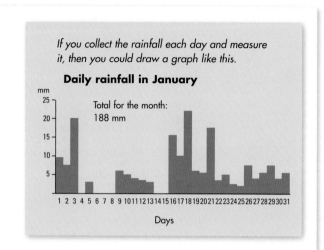

Daily rainfall in January

Total for the month: 188 mm

Days

Rainfall

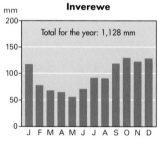

Inverewe

Total for the year: 1,128 mm

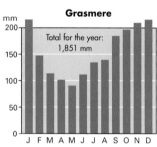

Grasmere

Total for the year: 1,851 mm

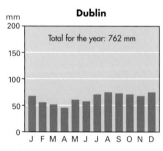

Dublin

Total for the year: 762 mm

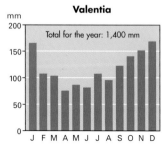

Valentia

Total for the year: 1,400 mm

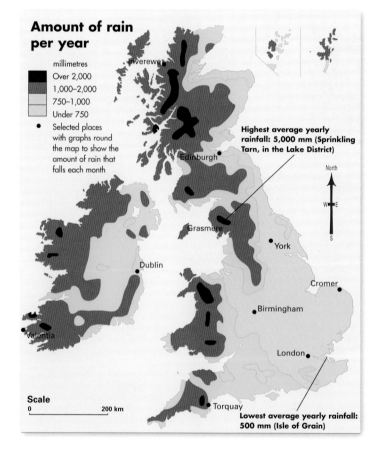

Amount of rain per year

millimetres
- Over 2,000
- 1,000–2,000
- 750–1,000
- Under 750
- Selected places with graphs round the map to show the amount of rain that falls each month

Highest average yearly rainfall: 5,000 mm (Sprinkling Tarn, in the Lake District)

Lowest average yearly rainfall: 500 mm (Isle of Grain)

North

Scale
0   200 km

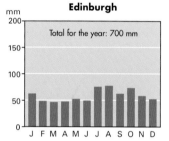

Edinburgh

Total for the year: 700 mm

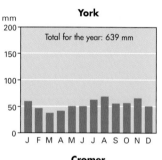

York

Total for the year: 639 mm

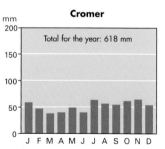

Cromer

Total for the year: 618 mm

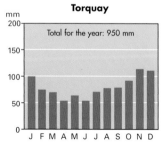

Torquay

Total for the year: 950 mm

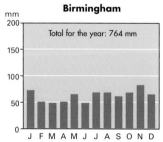

Birmingham

Total for the year: 764 mm

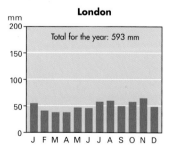

London

Total for the year: 593 mm

Wind

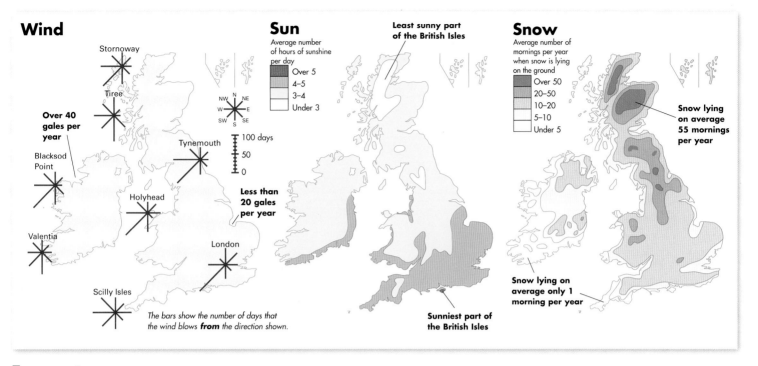

Stornoway
Tiree

Over 40 gales per year

Blacksod Point

Holyhead

Valentia

Tynemouth

London

Scilly Isles

Less than 20 gales per year

NW N NE
W E
SW S SE

100 days
50
0

*The bars show the number of days that the wind blows **from** the direction shown.*

Sun

Average number of hours of sunshine per day

- Over 5
- 4–5
- 3–4
- Under 3

Least sunny part of the British Isles

Sunniest part of the British Isles

Snow

Average number of mornings per year when snow is lying on the ground

- Over 50
- 20–50
- 10–20
- 5–10
- Under 5

Snow lying on average 55 mornings per year

Snow lying on average only 1 morning per year

Temperature

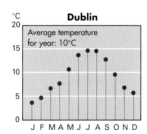
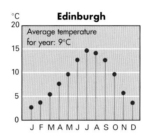
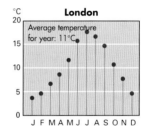
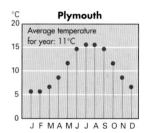
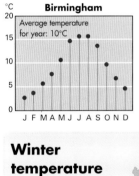

Birmingham — Average temperature for year: 10°C
Dublin — Average temperature for year: 10°C
Edinburgh — Average temperature for year: 9°C
London — Average temperature for year: 11°C
Plymouth — Average temperature for year: 11°C

(°C axis: 0, 5, 10, 15, 20; months: J F M A M J J A S O N D)

Winter temperature

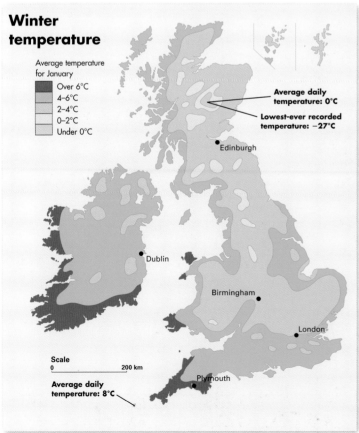

Average temperature for January

- Over 6°C
- 4–6°C
- 2–4°C
- 0–2°C
- Under 0°C

Average daily temperature: 0°C

Lowest-ever recorded temperature: −27°C

Edinburgh

Dublin

Birmingham

London

Scale
0   200 km

Average daily temperature: 8°C

Plymouth

Summer temperature

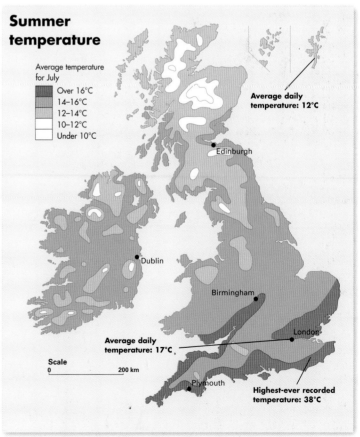

Average temperature for July

- Over 16°C
- 14–16°C
- 12–14°C
- 10–12°C
- Under 10°C

Average daily temperature: 12°C

Edinburgh

Dublin

Birmingham

Average daily temperature: 17°C

London

Scale
0   200 km

Plymouth

Highest-ever recorded temperature: 38°C

People, cities and towns

The UK Census

Every ten years, there is a government survey in the UK. The head of each household has to fill in a form. On the form, there are questions about the house and the people who live there. This is called the Census. The Census tells the government the number of people living in the UK. This helps the government to plan such things as schools and hospitals. The Census shows how the population has changed during the last century.

Here are some of the questions asked on the Census form:
How old are you?
Have you moved house in the last year?
In which country were you born?
To which ethnic group do you belong?
Have you a long-term illness?
Can you speak Welsh?
What do you do for a job?
How many hours a week do you work?
How do you get to work?
Where do you work?
Do you own or rent your house?
Do you have a bath, flush toilet or central heating?
Do you have a car?

People

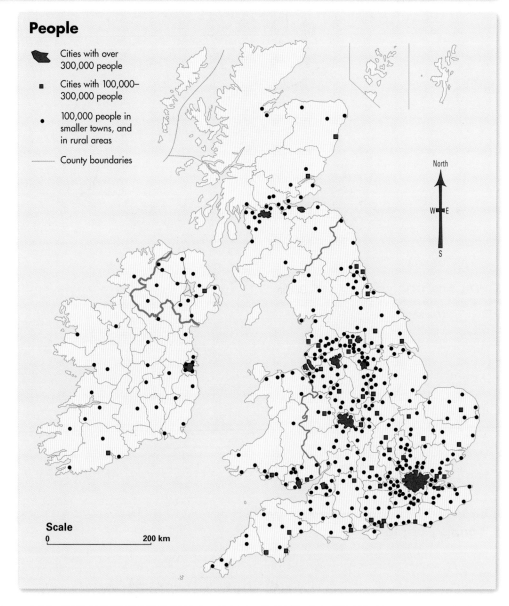

- Cities with over 300,000 people
- Cities with 100,000–300,000 people
- 100,000 people in smaller towns, and in rural areas
- County boundaries

Scale
0   200 km

Country population data

	1901	1951	2001
		millions	
England	30.5	41.2	49.2
Wales	2.0	2.6	2.9
Scotland	4.5	5.1	5.1
Northern Ireland	1.2	1.4	1.7
United Kingdom	**38.2**	**50.3**	**58.9**
Isle of Man	0.055	0.005	0.076
Channel Islands	0.096	0.102	0.147
Ireland	**3.2**	**2.9**	**3.9**

Changing numbers

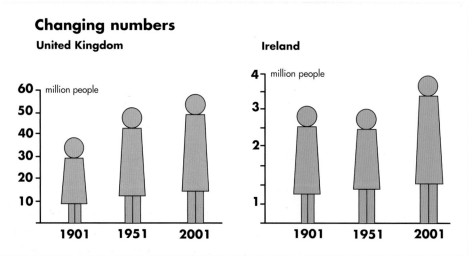

United Kingdom

million people

60
50
40
30
20
10

1901   1951   2001

Ireland

million people

4
3
2
1

1901   1951   2001

Cities

Cities with over 300,000 people

Cities with 100,000–300,000 people

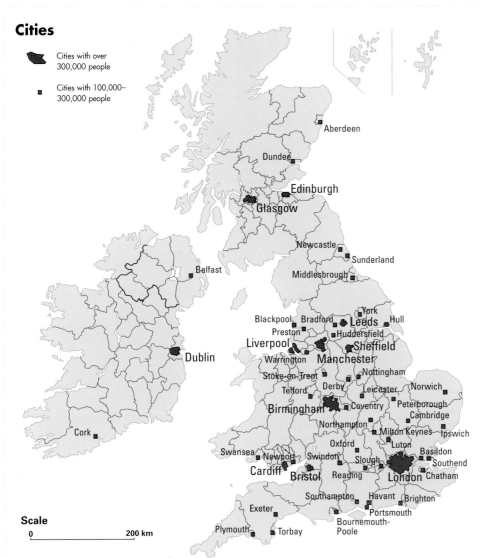

Scale

0 _____ 200 km

Population in 1981, 1991 and 2001

	1981	1991	2001
		thousand people	
London	**6,806**	**6,890**	**7,188**
Birmingham	**1,021**	**1,007**	**976**
Leeds	**718**	**717**	**716**
Glasgow	**774**	**689**	**579**
Sheffield	**548**	**529**	**513**
Edinburgh	**446**	**440**	**449**
Liverpool	**517**	**481**	**439**
Manchester	**463**	**439**	**393**
Bristol	**401**	**397**	**392**
Cardiff	**281**	**294**	**308**
Leicester	**283**	**285**	**287**
Nottingham	**278**	**281**	**284**
Belfast	**315**	**294**	**277**
Newcastle	**284**	**278**	**260**
Hull	**274**	**267**	**260**
Plymouth	**253**	**254**	**255**
Stoke-on-Trent	**252**	**253**	**254**
Dublin	**915**	**940**	**977**
Cork	**150**	**174**	**180**

These are the largest cities in the UK and Ireland. Note that very few increased their populations between 1981 and 2001.

Young people

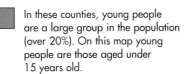

In these counties, young people are a large group in the population (over 20%). On this map young people are those aged under 15 years old.

In these counties, old people are a large group in the population (over 20%). On this map old people are women aged over 60 and men over 65 years old.

Look at these two maps. Can you think of some reasons why some counties have more older people than other counties?

Old people

11

Farming and fishing

Types of farm

Dairy farms
Cows for milk, butter and cheese

Beef farms
Cows and calves for beef and veal

Sheep farms
Sheep and lambs for wool and meat

Grain and root farms
Wheat, potatoes, sugar beet and oilseed rape

Mixed farms
Livestock and grain or roots

Market gardening
Vegetables, fruit and flowers

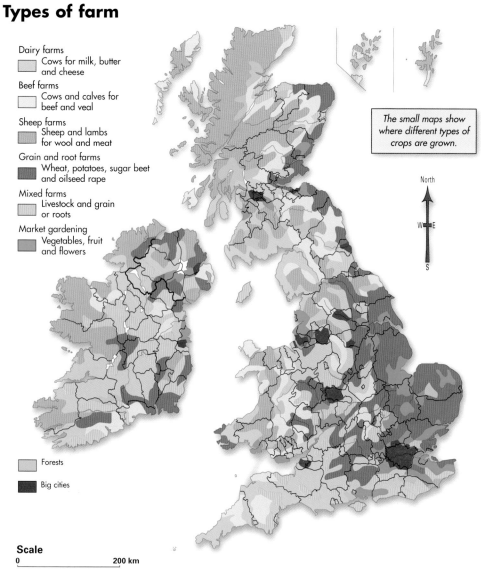

The small maps show where different types of crops are grown.

North

W—E

S

Forests

Big cities

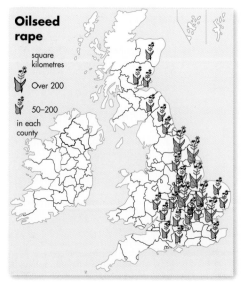

Scale

0   200 km

Wheat

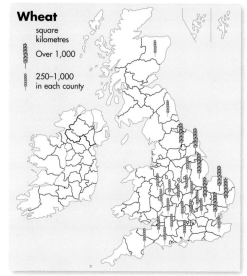

square kilometres

Over 1,000

250–1,000 in each county

Potatoes

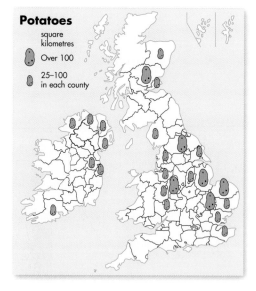

square kilometres

Over 100

25–100 in each county

Oilseed rape

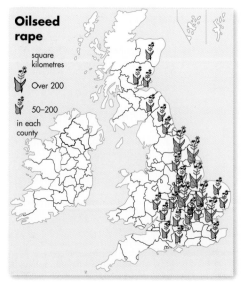

square kilometres

Over 200

50–200 in each county

Sugar beet

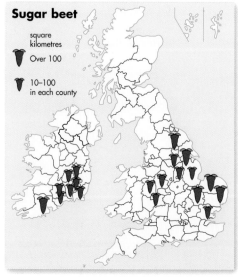

square kilometres

Over 100

10–100 in each county

Vegetables

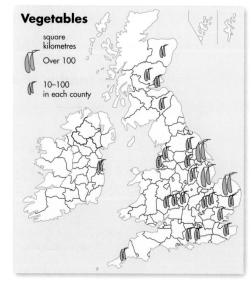

square kilometres

Over 100

10–100 in each county

Cattle

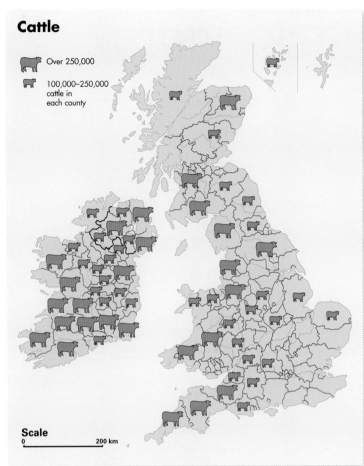

Over 250,000

100,000–250,000 cattle in each county

Scale
0   200 km

Sheep and pigs

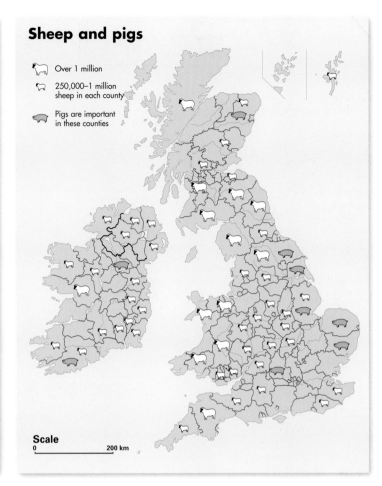

Over 1 million

250,000–1 million sheep in each county

Pigs are important in these counties

Scale
0   200 km

Land use in the UK

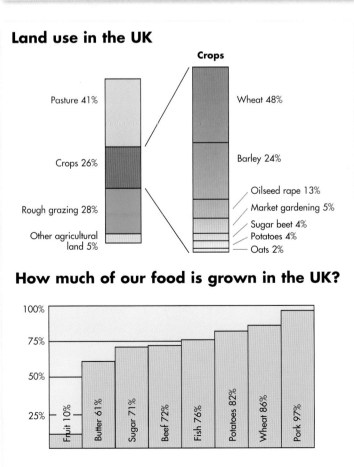

Crops

Pasture 41%

Crops 26%

Rough grazing 28%

Other agricultural land 5%

Wheat 48%

Barley 24%

Oilseed rape 13%

Market gardening 5%

Sugar beet 4%

Potatoes 4%

Oats 2%

How much of our food is grown in the UK?

100%
75%
50%
25%

Fruit 10%
Butter 61%
Sugar 71%
Beef 72%
Fish 76%
Potatoes 82%
Wheat 86%
Pork 97%

Fishing

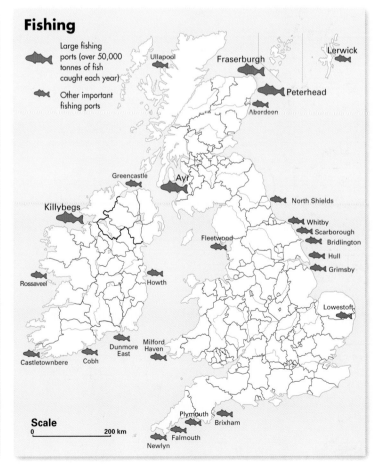

Large fishing ports (over 50,000 tonnes of fish caught each year)

Other important fishing ports

Ullapool
Fraserburgh
Lerwick
Peterhead
Aberdeen
Greencastle
Ayr
North Shields
Killybegs
Whitby
Scarborough
Fleetwood
Bridlington
Hull
Grimsby
Rossaveel
Howth
Lowestoft
Castletownbere
Cobh
Dunmore East
Milford Haven
Plymouth
Brixham
Falmouth
Newlyn

Scale
0   200 km

13

Total employment

The number of people working

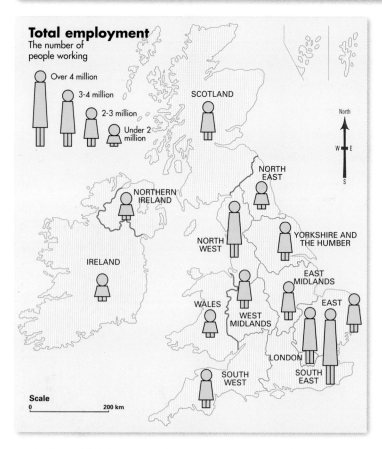

Over 4 million

3-4 million

2-3 million

Under 2 million

SCOTLAND

NORTHERN IRELAND

IRELAND

NORTH EAST

NORTH WEST

YORKSHIRE AND THE HUMBER

EAST MIDLANDS

WALES

WEST MIDLANDS

EAST

LONDON

SOUTH WEST

SOUTH EAST

North
W — E
S

Scale
0   200 km

Employment in services

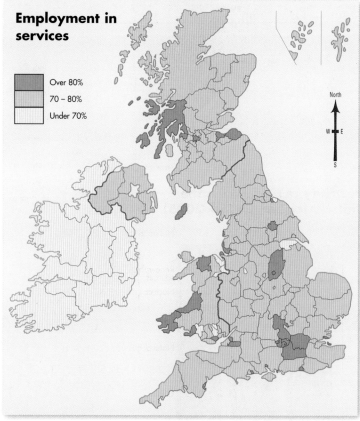

Over 80%

70 – 80%

Under 70%

North
W — E
S

Manufacturing industries are industries which make things. Some examples of manufactured goods are cars, steel, textiles and clothes.

Service industries do not make things. They provide a service to people. Shops, hotels and banks are examples of service industries.

Unemployment

% of the workforce who are unemployed

   5 – 6%   Over 6%

Employment in manufacturing

% of the workforce who are employed in manufacturing

   15 – 20%   Over 20%

Employment in agriculture

% of the workforce who are employed in agriculture, forestry and fishing

   2.5 – 10%   Over 10%

Sources of energy used in the United Kingdom

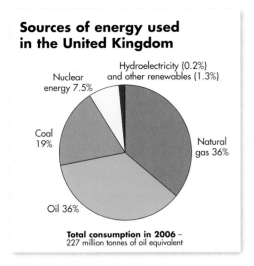

Nuclear energy 7.5%

Hydroelectricity (0.2%) and other renewables (1.3%)

Coal 19%

Natural gas 36%

Oil 36%

**Total consumption in 2006 –
227 million tonnes of oil equivalent**

Electricity generation in the United Kingdom (1980–2005)

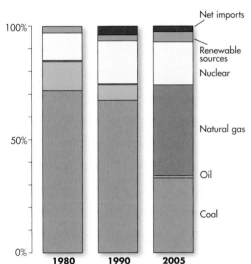

Net imports

Renewable sources

Nuclear

Natural gas

Oil

Coal

100%

50%

0%

1980   1990   2005

This bar-chart shows the different types of fuel that are used to make electricity in the UK. The use of coal and oil in the generation of electricity has dropped over the 25-year period from 1980 to 2005. However, the use of natural gas has increased by 40%.

Renewable energy

Renewable sources used to generate electricity (in million tonnes of oil equivalent)

	1998	2002	2006
Biofuels	0.9	1.8	3.2
Hydroelectricity	0.4	0.4	0.4
Wind Power	0.1	0.1	0.4
Total renewable energy	1.4	2.3	4.0

In 2006 4.5% of electricity in the UK was generated by renewable energy sources. The government aims to increase this to 10% by 2010 and 20% by 2020.

Energy sources in Great Britain and Ireland

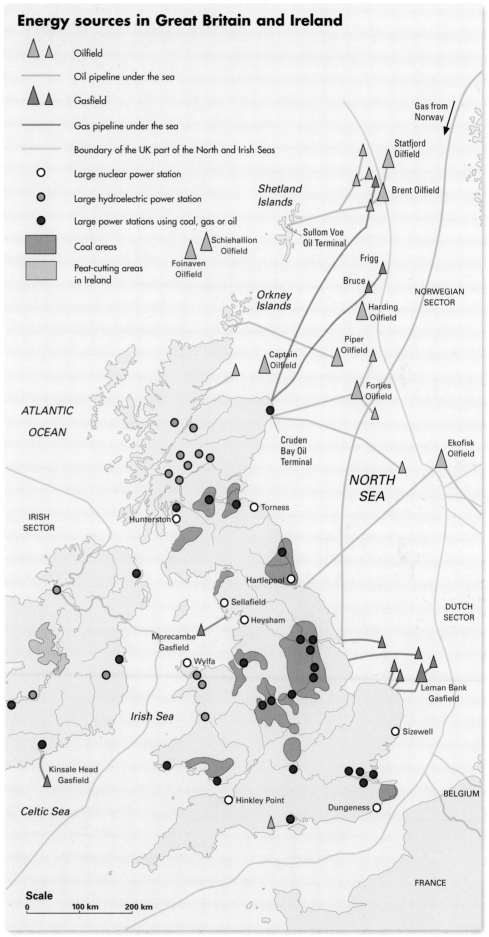

Oilfield

Oil pipeline under the sea

Gasfield

Gas pipeline under the sea

Boundary of the UK part of the North and Irish Seas

○ Large nuclear power station

◐ Large hydroelectric power station

● Large power stations using coal, gas or oil

Coal areas

Peat-cutting areas in Ireland

Gas from Norway

Statfjord Oilfield

Shetland Islands

Brent Oilfield

Sullom Voe Oil Terminal

Schiehallion Oilfield

Foinaven Oilfield

Frigg

Bruce

NORWEGIAN SECTOR

Harding Oilfield

Orkney Islands

Piper Oilfield

Captain Oilfield

Forties Oilfield

ATLANTIC OCEAN

Cruden Bay Oil Terminal

NORTH SEA

Ekofisk Oilfield

Torness

Hunterston

IRISH SECTOR

Hartlepool

DUTCH SECTOR

Sellafield

Heysham

Morecambe Gasfield

Wylfa

Leman Bank Gasfield

Irish Sea

Sizewell

Kinsale Head Gasfield

Hinkley Point

Dungeness

BELGIUM

Celtic Sea

FRANCE

Scale

0   100 km   200 km

15

Transport

There are about 380 thousand kilometres of road in the UK. The total number of cars, buses, lorries and motorbikes is 26 million. That is almost half the number of people in the UK. The maps on this page show the motorways and some main roads in the UK and the number of cars in the different regions. At the bottom of the page there are tables showing the road distances between important towns.

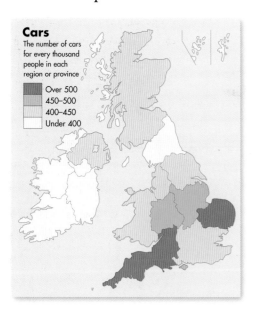

Cars
The number of cars for every thousand people in each region or province

- Over 500
- 450–500
- 400–450
- Under 400

Roads

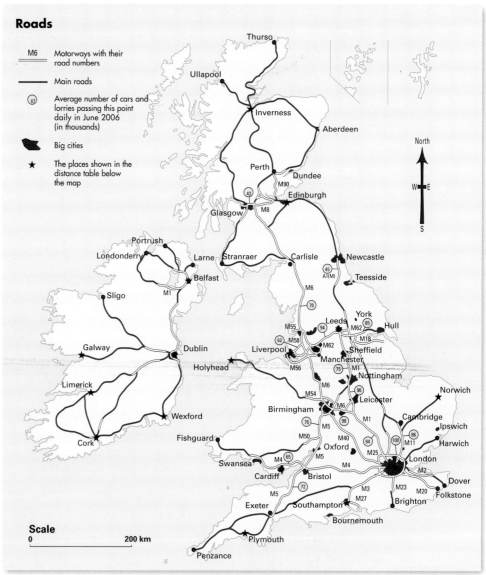

M6 — Motorways with their road numbers

— Main roads

(67) — Average number of cars and lorries passing this point daily in June 2006 (in thousands)

— Big cities

★ — The places shown in the distance table below the map

Scale
0 — 200 km

UK	Birmingham	Cardiff	Edinburgh	Holyhead	Inverness	Leeds	Liverpool	London	Manchester	Norwich	Plymouth	Southampton
Birmingham		163	460	246	716	179	151	179	130	249	320	206
Cardiff	163		587	341	843	341	264	249	277	381	259	192
Edinburgh	460	587		489	256	320	338	608	336	586	790	669
Holyhead	246	341	489		745	262	151	420	198	481	528	455
Inverness	716	843	256	745		579	605	864	604	842	1049	925
Leeds	179	341	320	262	579		119	306	64	277	502	378
Liverpool	151	264	338	151	605	119		330	55	360	452	357
London	179	249	608	420	864	306	330		309	172	343	127
Manchester	130	277	336	198	604	64	55	309		306	457	325
Norwich	249	381	586	481	842	277	360	172	306		515	299
Plymouth	320	259	790	528	1049	502	452	343	457	515		246
Southampton	206	192	669	455	925	378	357	127	325	299	246	

Road distances

The distance tables are in kilometres, but distances on road signposts in the UK are in miles.
A mile is longer than a kilometre.
1 mile = 1.6 kilometres. 1 kilometre = 0.6 mile.

Ireland	Belfast	Cork	Dublin	Galway	Limerick	Wexford
Belfast		418	160	300	222	306
Cork	418		257	193	97	190
Dublin	160	257		210	193	137
Galway	300	193	210		97	249
Limerick	222	97	193	97		193
Wexford	306	190	137	249	193	

Railways

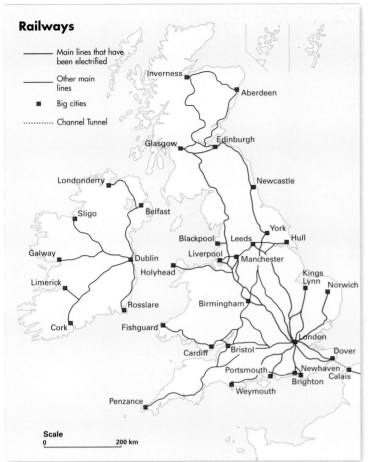

- Main lines that have been electrified
- Other main lines
- ■ Big cities
- Channel Tunnel

Inverness
Aberdeen
Glasgow
Edinburgh
Newcastle
Londonderry
Sligo
Belfast
York
Hull
Galway
Blackpool
Leeds
Liverpool
Manchester
Dublin
Holyhead
Kings Lynn
Norwich
Limerick
Rosslare
Birmingham
Cork
Fishguard
London
Cardiff
Bristol
Dover
Portsmouth
Newhaven
Calais
Brighton
Weymouth
Penzance

Scale
0   200 km

Manchester – the daily flow of people

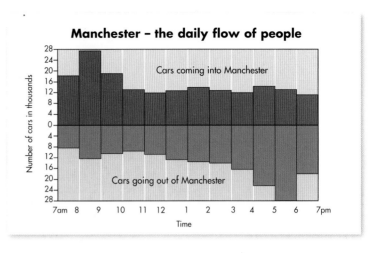

Number of cars in thousands

Cars coming into Manchester

Cars going out of Manchester

7am 8 9 10 11 12 1 2 3 4 5 6 7pm

Time

High speed rail

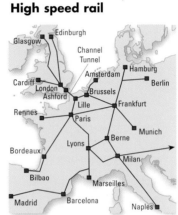

Edinburgh
Glasgow
Channel Tunnel
Amsterdam
Hamburg
Cardiff
Berlin
London
Ashford
Brussels
Rennes
Lille
Frankfurt
Paris
Munich
Berne
Bordeaux
Lyons
Bilbao
Milan
Marseilles
Madrid
Barcelona
Naples

By the year 2010 trains will be able to travel at over 200km/h on those lines shown on the map.

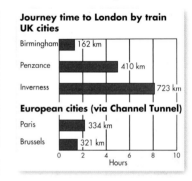

Journey time to London by train UK cities

Birmingham 162 km
Penzance 410 km
Inverness 723 km

European cities (via Channel Tunnel)

Paris 334 km
Brussels 321 km

0 2 4 6 8 10
Hours

Ports and ferries

- Major ports
- Other ports
- These ports are handling mainly fuel
- Important canals and rivers carrying goods
- Ferries

Orkney Is.
Sullom Voe
Ullapool
Orkney
Cromarty Firth
Peterhead
Shetland Is.
Caledonian Canal
Aberdeen
Glensanda
Dundee
Oban
Clyde
Forth
Ayr
Blyth
Norway, Sweden, Denmark
Cairnryan
Tyne
Larne
Stranraer
Sunderland
Tees and Hartlepool
Belfast
Sligo
Heysham
Warrenpoint
Fleetwood
Aire & Calder
Hull
Drogheda
Netherlands, Belgium
Dublin
Liverpool
Goole
Manchester
Grimsby and Immingham
Holyhead
Manchester Ship Canal
Boston
Limerick
New Ross
River Trent
Kings Lynn
River Yare
Great Yarmouth
Foynes
Waterford
Rosslare
Felixstowe
Bantry Bay
Cork
Fishguard
Ipswich
River Severn
Harwich
Neth., Belg.
Swansea
Newport
Ramsgate
Milford Haven
Port Talbot
Bristol
London
Medway
Dover
Cardiff
France
Southampton
Folkestone
Poole
Shoreham
Portsmouth
Newhaven
Fowey
Plymouth
Channel Is.
France
Scilly Isles
Spain France

Scale
0   200 km

Airports

- ✈ Over half the people are travelling within the UK or Ireland (Domestic airports)
- ✈ Over half the people are travelling to other countries (International airports)

Aberdeen
Glasgow
Edinburgh
Prestwick
Newcastle
Belfast
Durham/Tees Valley
Isle of Man
Leeds/Bradford
Liverpool
Doncaster/Sheffield
Manchester
Dublin
Nottingham East Midlands
Shannon
Birmingham
Luton
Cork
Bristol
Stansted
Cardiff
London City
Heathrow
Gatwick
Southampton
Bournemouth
Exeter

Scale
0   200 km

Conservation and tourism

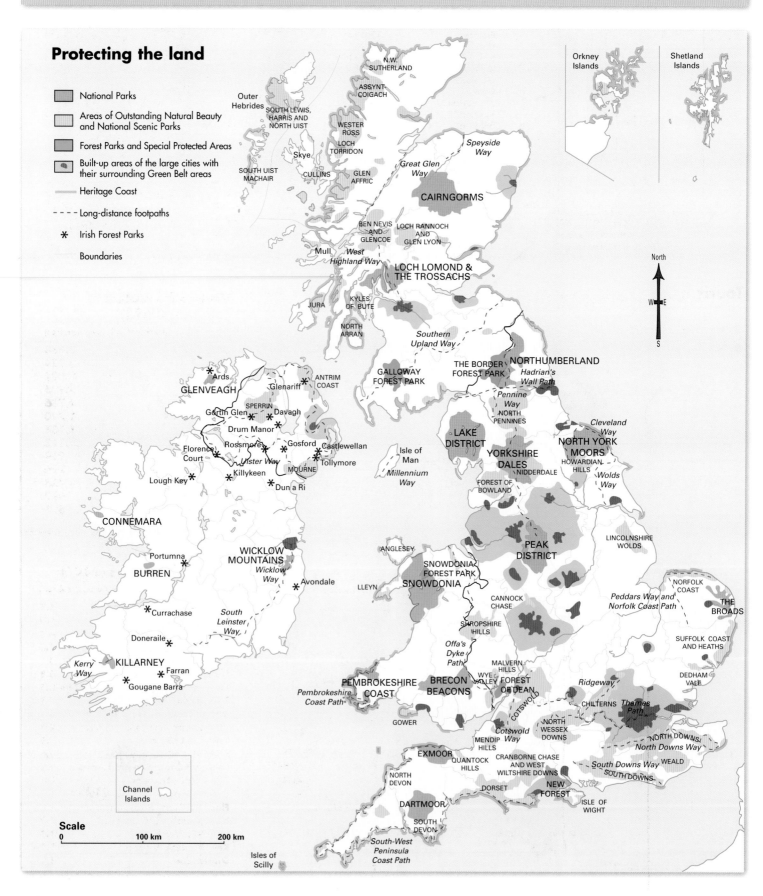

Protecting the land

Legend:
- National Parks
- Areas of Outstanding Natural Beauty and National Scenic Parks
- Forest Parks and Special Protected Areas
- Built-up areas of the large cities with their surrounding Green Belt areas
- Heritage Coast
- Long-distance footpaths
- ✳ Irish Forest Parks
- Boundaries

Orkney Islands

Shetland Islands

N.W. SUTHERLAND
ASSYNT-COIGACH
Outer Hebrides
SOUTH LEWIS, HARRIS AND NORTH UIST
WESTER ROSS
LOCH TORRIDON
Skye
Speyside Way
Great Glen Way
SOUTH UIST MACHAIR
CULLINS
GLEN AFFRIC
CAIRNGORMS
BEN NEVIS AND GLENCOE
LOCH RANNOCH AND GLEN LYON
Mull
West Highland Way
LOCH LOMOND & THE TROSSACHS
JURA
KYLES OF BUTE
NORTH ARRAN
Southern Upland Way
GALLOWAY FOREST PARK

North
W E
S

*Ards
GLENVEAGH
Glenariff
ANTRIM COAST
*Gortin Glen
SPERRIN
*Davagh
Drum Manor
*Rossmore
*Gosford *Castlewellan
Florence Court
Ulster Way
MOURNE *Tollymore
*Killykeen
Lough Key *
*Dun a Ri

THE BORDER FOREST PARK
NORTHUMBERLAND
Hadrian's Wall Path
Pennine Way
NORTH PENNINES
LAKE DISTRICT
Isle of Man
Millennium Way
Cleveland Way
NORTH YORK MOORS
HOWARDIAN HILLS
Wolds Way
YORKSHIRE DALES
NIDDERDALE
FOREST OF BOWLAND

CONNEMARA
Portumna
BURREN
WICKLOW MOUNTAINS
Wicklow Way
*Avondale
*Currachase
South Leinster Way
Doneraile *
Kerry Way
KILLARNEY
*Farran
*Gougane Barra

ANGLESEY
SNOWDONIA FOREST PARK
SNOWDONIA
LLEYN
CANNOCK CHASE
SHROPSHIRE HILLS
Offa's Dyke Path
PEAK DISTRICT
LINCOLNSHIRE WOLDS
NORFOLK COAST
Peddars Way and Norfolk Coast Path
THE BROADS
SUFFOLK COAST AND HEATHS

PEMBROKESHIRE COAST
Pembrokeshire Coast Path
BRECON BEACONS
Wye Valley
MALVERN HILLS
FOREST OF DEAN
Cotswold Way
COTSWOLD
Ridgeway
CHILTERNS
Thames Path
DEDHAM VALE
GOWER
MENDIP HILLS
NORTH WESSEX DOWNS
NORTH DOWNS
North Downs Way
WEALD

EXMOOR
QUANTOCK HILLS
CRANBORNE CHASE AND WEST WILTSHIRE DOWNS
South Downs Way
SOUTH DOWNS
NORTH DEVON
DORSET
NEW FOREST
ISLE OF WIGHT
DARTMOOR
SOUTH DEVON
South-West Peninsula Coast Path

Channel Islands

Scale
0   100 km   200 km

Isles of Scilly

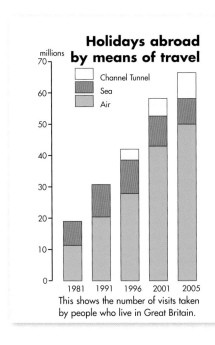

Holidays abroad by means of travel

millions

Legend:
- Channel Tunnel
- Sea
- Air

Years: 1981, 1991, 1996, 2001, 2005

This shows the number of visits taken by people who live in Great Britain.

British tourists to other countries (2005)

(number of tourists in thousands)

Spain	13,837
France	11,094
USA	4,241
Ireland	4,221
Italy	3,374
Germany	2,493
Greece	2,435
Netherlands	2,174
Portugal	1,855
Belgium	1,733
Cyprus	1,431
Turkey	1,367
Switzerland	1,001
Czech Republic	786

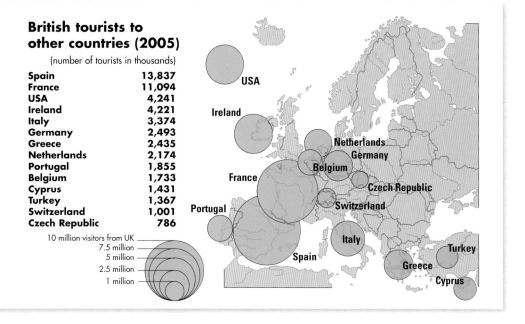

10 million visitors from UK
7.5 million
5 million
2.5 million
1 million

Tourism

- ● Main holiday cities and towns
- ● Major tourist attractions

Scale
0 — 200 km

Visitors from other countries (2005)

(number of visitors in thousands)

USA	3,438
France	3,324
Germany	3,294
Ireland	2,806
Spain	1,786
Netherlands	1,720
Italy	1,186
Belgium	1,112
Australia	919
Canada	796
Sweden	728
Switzerland	699
Norway	627

Tourist attractions (2006)

(number of visitors in millions)

Blackpool Pleasure Beach	5.7
Tate Modern, London	4.9
British Museum, London	4.8
National Gallery, London	4.6
British Airways London Eye	4.1
Natural History Museum, London	3.8
River Lee Country Park, Hertfordshire	3.5
Xscape, Castleford	3.5
Science Museum, London	2.4
Victoria and Albert Museum, London	2.4
Tower of London	2.1
St Paul's Cathedral, London	1.6
Natural Portrait Gallery, London	1.6
Tate Britain, London	1.6
Great Yarmouth Pleasure Beach	1.4
Flamingo Land, Kirby Misperton	1.3
New Metroland, Gateshead	1.3
Lake Windermere	1.3
Kew Gardens, London	1.2
Chester Zoo	1.2

Water

Rainfall areas – wet and dry

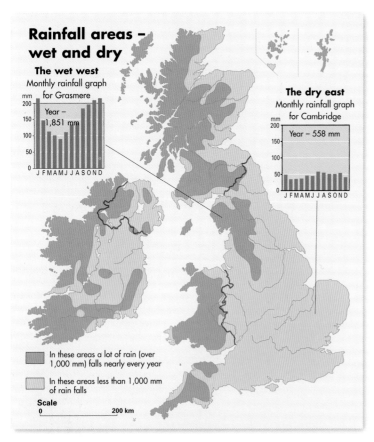

The wet west
Monthly rainfall graph for Grasmere

Year – 1,851 mm

mm
200
150
100
50
0
J F M A M J J A S O N D

The dry east
Monthly rainfall graph for Cambridge

Year – 558 mm

mm
200
150
100
50
0
J F M A M J J A S O N D

In these areas a lot of rain (over 1,000 mm) falls nearly every year

In these areas less than 1,000 mm of rain falls

Scale
0   200 km

Reservoirs and boreholes

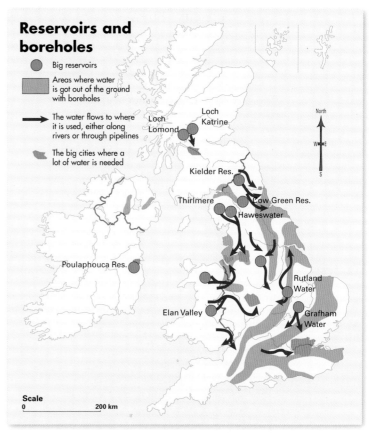

- Big reservoirs
- Areas where water is got out of the ground with boreholes
- The water flows to where it is used, either along rivers or through pipelines
- The big cities where a lot of water is needed

North
W E
S

Loch Lomond
Loch Katrine
Kielder Res.
Thirlmere
Cow Green Res.
Haweswater
Poulaphouca Res.
Rutland Water
Elan Valley
Grafham Water

Scale
0   200 km

Sources of river pollution

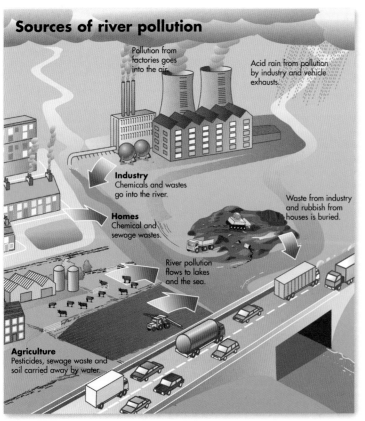

Pollution from factories goes into the air

Acid rain from pollution by industry and vehicle exhausts.

Industry
Chemicals and wastes go into the river.

Waste from industry and rubbish from houses is buried.

Homes
Chemical and sewage wastes.

River pollution flows to lakes and the sea.

Agriculture
Pesticides, sewage waste and soil carried away by water.

River pollution

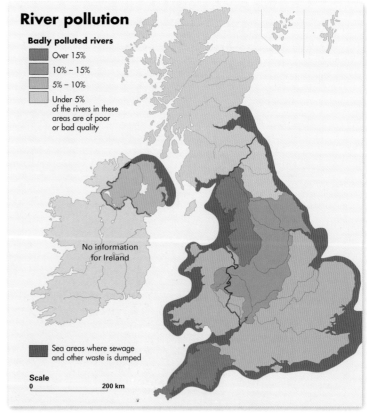

Badly polluted rivers

- Over 15%
- 10% – 15%
- 5% – 10%
- Under 5%
  of the rivers in these areas are of poor or bad quality

No information for Ireland

Sea areas where sewage and other waste is dumped

Scale
0   200 km

The average UK household uses 355 litres of water a day. Up to 135,000 million litres of water are used each day in the UK. Over half the water is used by people in their homes. About a third is used to make electricity. The rest is used in farms and factories. On the right are some of the ways that water is used in the home:

To make one car can use up to 30,000 litres of water. To brew one pint of beer needs 8 pints of water.

Domestic appliances – water usage

	(per wash)
Washing machine	80 litres
Bath	80 litres
Dishwasher	35 litres
Shower	35 litres
Toilet flush	6 litres

Flooding

Around 5 million people, in 2 million properties, live in flood risk areas in England and Wales. In summer 2007 there were several periods of extreme rainfall which led to widespread flooding.

The Environment Agency has an important role in warning people about the risk of flooding, and in reducing the likelihood of flooding from rivers and the sea.

Flood risk in England and Wales

- Areas at greatest risk from flooding
- Counties worst affected by flooding in summer 2007

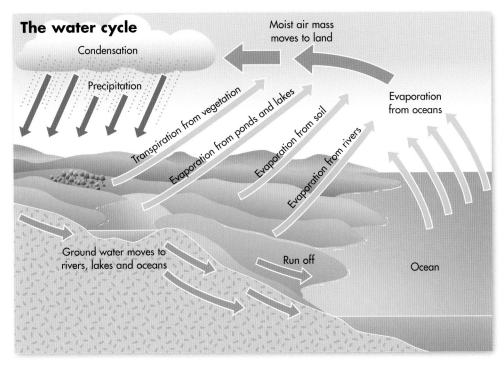

The water cycle

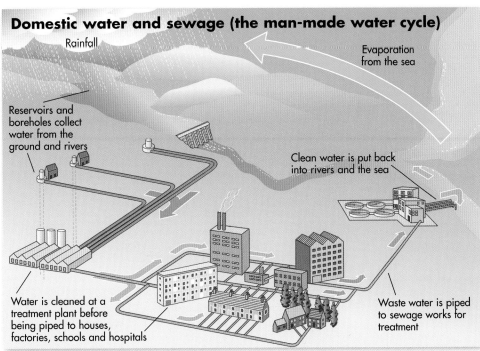

Domestic water and sewage (the man-made water cycle)

Counties and regions

Names

*The map on the left shows the **British Isles**, which is made up of the two large islands of **Great Britain** and **Ireland** and many smaller islands. There are two countries, the **United Kingdom** and **Ireland**. The full name of the United Kingdom is The United Kingdom of Great Britain and Northern Ireland. It has four parts: **England**, **Wales**, **Scotland** and **Northern Ireland**. It is known for short as the United Kingdom, UK or Britain. The whole country is often wrongly called England. The Republic of Ireland is sometimes shown as Eire (on its stamps), which is the name of Ireland in the Irish language.*

These are the names for some of the different areas in the British Isles

Counties and regions

The map shows the Standard Regions of the United Kingdom. The boundaries follow those of the counties shown on page 23. Large bodies like the Health Service, Water or Electricity divide the country up into their own regions. Ireland is divided into four historic provinces.

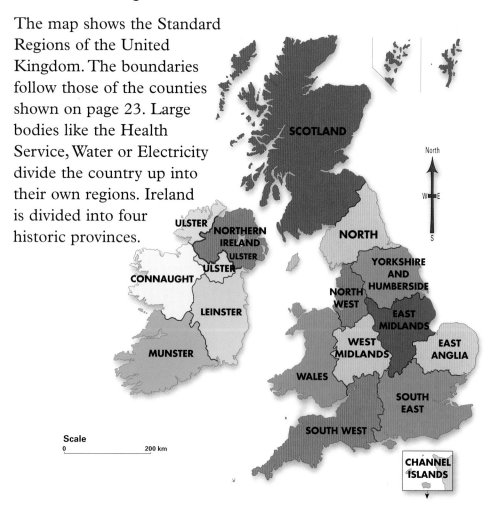

Counties and unitary authorities

England and Wales are divided into counties, unitary authorities and boroughs. The counties are divided into districts, and the districts into parishes and wards. Scotland is divided into regions and unitary authorities, and Northern Ireland into districts.

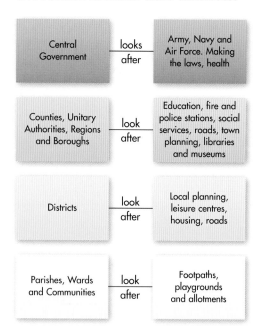

Central Government	looks after	Army, Navy and Air Force. Making the laws, health
Counties, Unitary Authorities, Regions and Boroughs	look after	Education, fire and police stations, social services, roads, town planning, libraries and museums
Districts	look after	Local planning, leisure centres, housing, roads
Parishes, Wards and Communities	look after	Footpaths, playgrounds and allotments

Area data

	Area in square kilometres
England	130,439
Wales	20,768
Scotland	77,167
Northern Ireland	13,483
United Kingdom	**241,857**
Isle of Man	**572**
Channel Islands	**195**
Ireland	**68,896**

The Channel Islands and the Isle of Man are dependencies of the Crown and have their own parliaments. They are not part of the United Kingdom.

The six counties are shown in Northern Ireland. It is divided for local government into 26 districts.

The map shows the 6 counties in Northern Ireland, the 32 unitary authorities in Scotland, the 22 unitary authorities in Wales, and the 87 unitary authorities in England as of 1 April 1998. Authorities which are too small to name on the map are numbered and listed separately.

SCOTLAND
1. ABERDEEN CITY
2. DUNDEE CITY
3. WEST DUNBARTONSHIRE
4. EAST DUNBARTONSHIRE
5. CITY OF GLASGOW
6. INVERCLYDE
7. RENFREWSHIRE
8. EAST RENFREWSHIRE
9. NORTH LANARKSHIRE
10. FALKIRK
11. CLACKMANNANSHIRE
12. WEST LOTHIAN
13. CITY OF EDINBURGH
14. MIDLOTHIAN

WALES
15. SWANSEA
16. NEATH PORT TALBOT
17. BRIDGEND
18. RHONDDA CYNON TAFF
19. MERTHYR TYDFIL
20. CAERPHILLY
21. BLAENAU GWENT
22. TORFAEN
23. CARDIFF
24. NEWPORT

ENGLAND
25. HARTLEPOOL
26. DARLINGTON
27. STOCKTON-ON-TEES
28. MIDDLESBROUGH
29. REDCAR AND CLEVELAND
30. BLACKPOOL
31. BLACKBURN WITH DARWEN
32. HALTON
33. WARRINGTON
34. KINGSTON UPON HULL
35. NORTH EAST LINCOLNSHIRE
36. STOKE-ON-TRENT
37. TELFORD AND WREKIN
38. DERBY CITY
39. CITY OF NOTTINGHAM
40. LEICESTER CITY
41. RUTLAND
42. PETERBOROUGH
43. MILTON KEYNES
44. LUTON
45. NORTH SOMERSET
46. CITY OF BRISTOL
47. BATH AND N. E. SOMERSET
48. SWINDON
49. READING
50. WOKINGHAM
51. WINDSOR AND MAIDENHEAD
52. SLOUGH
53. BRACKNELL FOREST
54. THURROCK
55. SOUTHEND-ON-SEA
56. MEDWAY
57. PLYMOUTH
58. TORBAY
59. POOLE
60. BOURNEMOUTH
61. SOUTHAMPTON
62. PORTSMOUTH
63. BRIGHTON AND HOVE

Capital cities

Scale
0   100 km   200 km

23

England and Wales

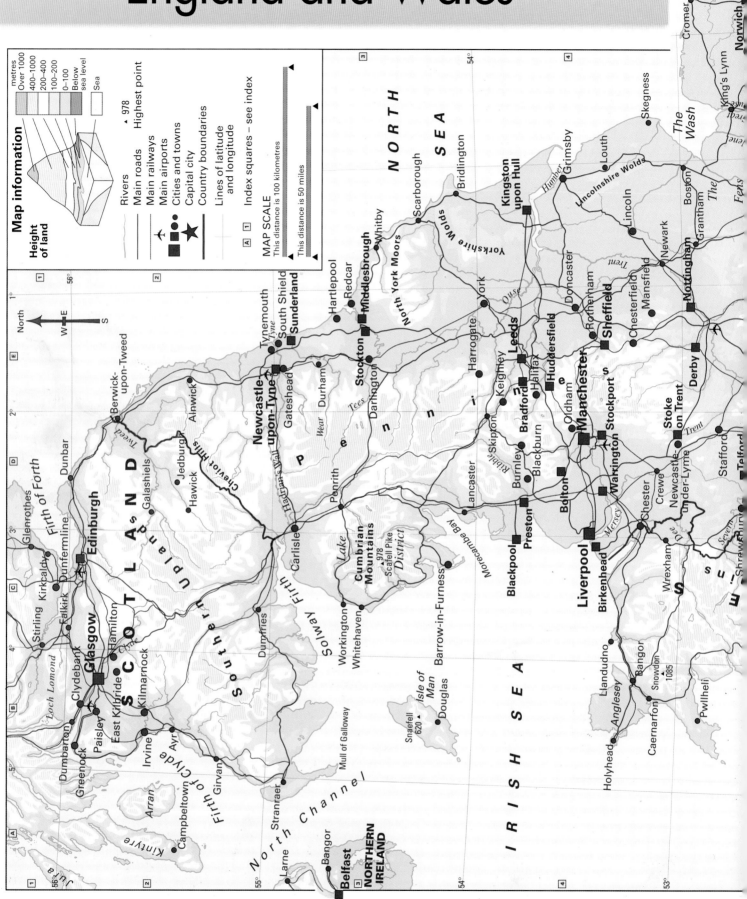

Map information

Height of land

metres	
	Over 1000
	400–1000
	200–400
	100–200
	0–100
	Below sea level
	Sea

▲ 978 Highest point

Rivers
Main roads
Main railways
✈ Main airports
● Cities and towns
★ Capital city
Country boundaries
Lines of latitude and longitude

A1 Index squares – see index

MAP SCALE
This distance is 100 kilometres
This distance is 50 miles

NORTH SEA

IRISH SEA

North Channel

SCOTLAND

NORTHERN IRELAND

Southern Uplands

Cheviot Hills

Pennines

Cumbrian Mountains
Lake District
978 Scafell Pike

Yorkshire Wolds

North York Moors

Lincolnshire Wolds

The Wash

The Fens

Snowdon 1085

Anglesey

Snaefell 620
Isle of Man

Firth of Forth
Firth of Clyde
Solway Firth
Morecambe Bay

Glasgow, Edinburgh, Newcastle upon-Tyne, Sunderland, Middlesbrough, Manchester, Liverpool, Leeds, Sheffield, Bradford, Nottingham, Kingston upon Hull, Norwich

Berwick-upon-Tweed, Dunbar, Glenrothes, Dunfermline, Kirkcaldy, Stirling, Falkirk, Hamilton, Clydebank, East Kilbride, Paisley, Greenock, Dumbarton, Irvine, Kilmarnock, Ayr, Girvan, Stranraer, Dumfries, Carlisle, Penrith, Workington, Whitehaven, Barrow-in-Furness, Lancaster, Preston, Blackpool, Blackburn, Burnley, Bolton, Warrington, Birkenhead, Chester, Crewe, Stoke on Trent, Newcastle-under-Lyme, Stafford, Telford, Shrewsbury, Wrexham, Bangor, Llandudno, Holyhead, Caernarfon, Pwllheli, Douglas

Alnwick, Jedburgh, Hawick, Galashiels, Durham, Gateshead, South Shields, Tynemouth, Hartlepool, Redcar, Stockton, Darlington, Whitby, Scarborough, Bridlington, York, Harrogate, Skipton, Keighley, Halifax, Huddersfield, Oldham, Stockport, Rotherham, Chesterfield, Mansfield, Newark, Derby, Doncaster, Grimsby, Louth, Lincoln, Boston, Grantham, Skegness, King's Lynn, Cromer, Great Yarmouth

Belfast, Bangor, Larne

Arran, Jura, Kintyre, Campbeltown, Mull of Galloway

Tweed, Tyne, Wear, Tees, Ouse, Humber, Trent, Severn, Dee, Mersey, Ribble, Hadrian's Wall

Loch Lomond

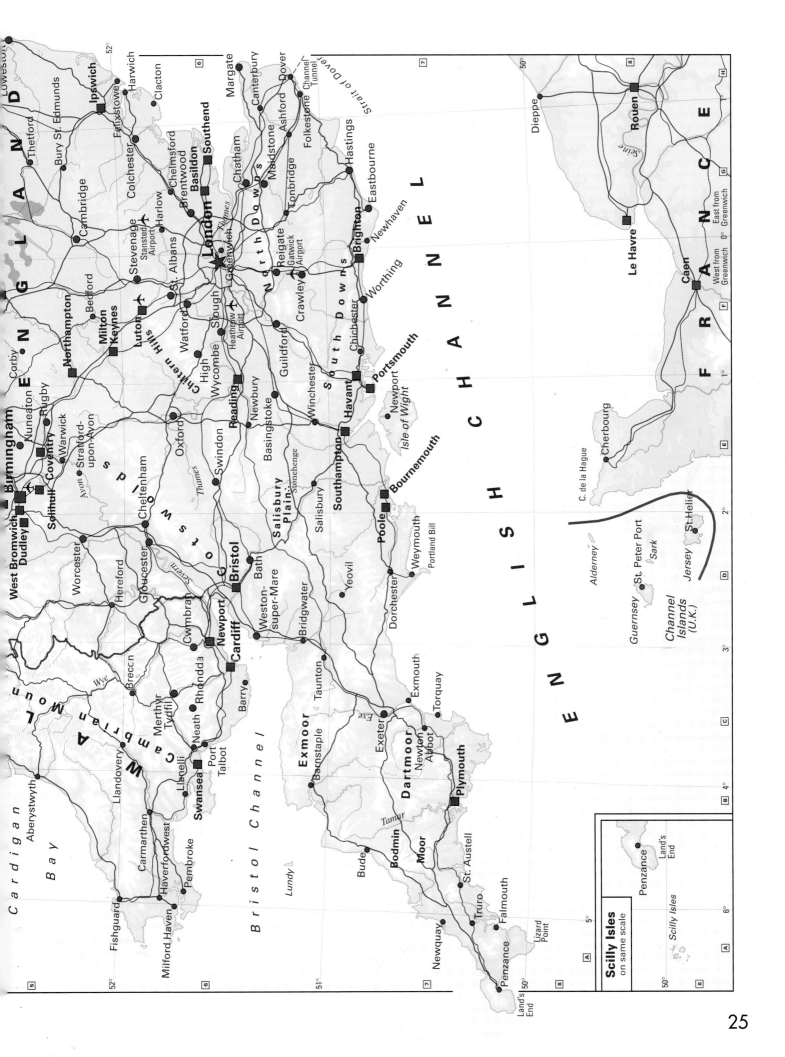

25

Scotland and Ireland

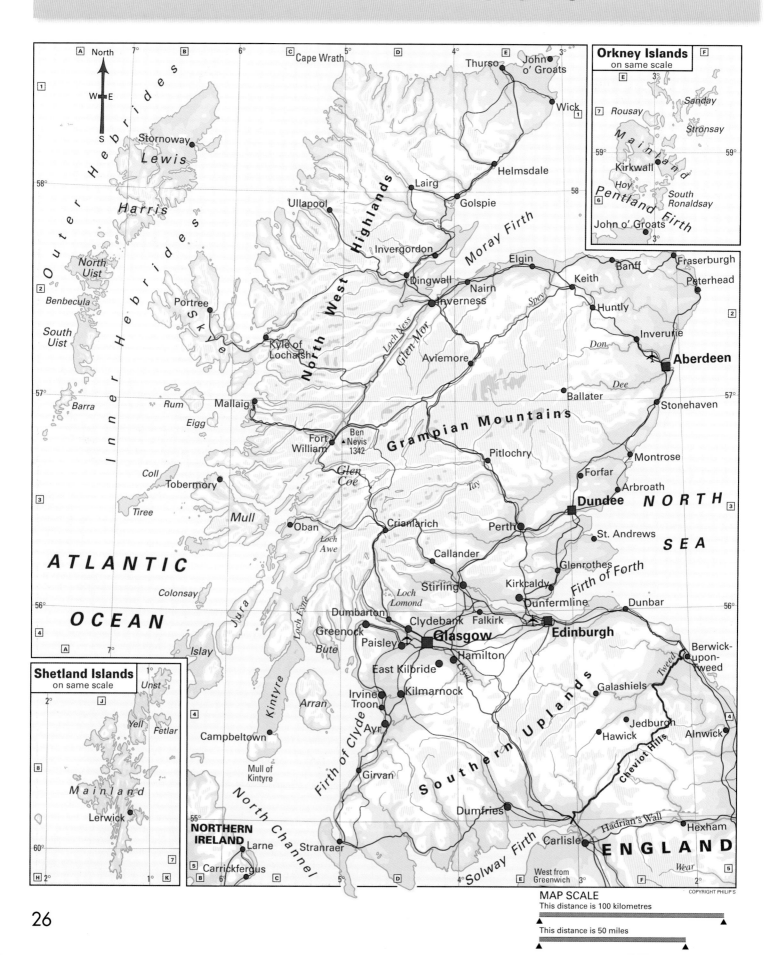

Orkney Islands on same scale

Rousay · Sanday · Stronsay · Mainland · Kirkwall · Hoy · South Ronaldsay · Pentland Firth · John o' Groats

Shetland Islands on same scale

Unst · Yell · Fetlar · Mainland · Lerwick

North
W E
S

Cape Wrath · Thurso · John o' Groats · Wick · Stornoway · Lewis · Harris · Outer Hebrides · North Uist · Benbecula · South Uist · Barra · Inner Hebrides · Skye · Portree · Kyle of Lochalsh · Helmsdale · Lairg · Ullapool · Golspie · Invergordon · North West Highlands · Dingwall · Nairn · Inverness · Elgin · Keith · Banff · Fraserburgh · Peterhead · Huntly · Moray Firth · Spey · Inverurie · Aviemore · Loch Ness · Glen Mor · Don · Aberdeen · Mallaig · Rum · Eigg · Fort William · Ben Nevis 1342 · Grampian Mountains · Dee · Ballater · Stonehaven · Coll · Tobermory · Glen Coe · Tiree · Mull · Tay · Pitlochry · Montrose · Forfar · Arbroath · Oban · Loch Awe · Crianlarich · Perth · Dundee · NORTH · St. Andrews · Callander · Colonsay · Glenrothes · Firth of Forth · SEA · Stirling · Kirkcaldy · Loch Lomond · Dunfermline · Dunbar · Dumbarton · Clydebank · Falkirk · Greenock · Paisley · Glasgow · Edinburgh · Bute · Hamilton · Berwick-upon-Tweed · East Kilbride · Kilmarnock · Tweed · Galashiels · Islay · Irvine · Troon · Jura · Arran · Ayr · Jedburgh · Alnwick · Campbeltown · Kintyre · Hawick · Cheviot Hills · Southern Uplands · Mull of Kintyre · Girvan · Firth of Clyde · Dumfries · Hadrian's Wall · Hexham · Carlisle · ENGLAND · NORTHERN IRELAND · Larne · Stranraer · North Channel · Solway Firth · Wear · Carrickfergus · West from Greenwich

ATLANTIC OCEAN

Loch Fyne

MAP SCALE
This distance is 100 kilometres

This distance is 50 miles

COPYRIGHT PHILIP'S

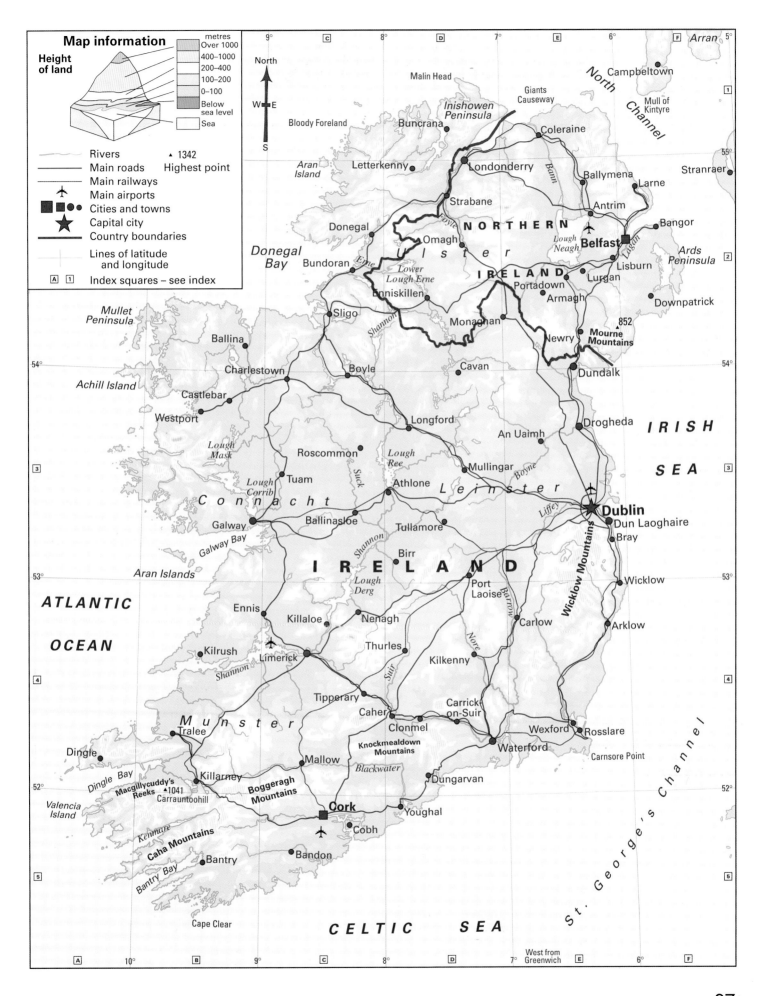

Map information

Height of land

	metres
	Over 1000
	400–1000
	200–400
	100–200
	0–100
	Below sea level
	Sea

Rivers

Main roads   ▲ 1342 Highest point

Main railways

✈ Main airports

■ ■ ● ● Cities and towns

★ Capital city

Country boundaries

Lines of latitude and longitude

Ⓐ ① Index squares – see index

North
W◼E
S

Arran

North Channel

Campbeltown

Malin Head

Giants Causeway

Mull of Kintyre

Inishowen Peninsula

Buncrana

Coleraine

Stranraer

Bloody Foreland

Letterkenny

Londonderry

Ballymena

Larne

Aran Island

Strabane

Antrim

Bangor

Donegal

N O R T H E R N

Omagh

Lough Neagh

Belfast

Ards Peninsula

Donegal Bay

U l s t e r

I R E L A N D

Lisburn

Bundoran

Lower Lough Erne

Portadown

Lurgan

Enniskillen

Armagh

Downpatrick

Mullet Peninsula

Sligo

Shannon

Monaghan

Newry

852

Mourne Mountains

Ballina

Cavan

Dundalk

IRISH

Charlestown

Boyle

Achill Island

Castlebar

Longford

Drogheda

Westport

An Uaimh

SEA

Lough Mask

Roscommon

Lough Ree

Mullingar

Boyne

Lough Corrib

Tuam

Suck

Athlone

L e i n s t e r

C o n n a c h t

Galway

Ballinasloe

Liffey

Dublin

Galway Bay

Tullamore

Dun Laoghaire

Bray

Aran Islands

I R E L A N D

Birr

Shannon

Wicklow Mountains

Ennis

Lough Derg

Port Laoise

Wicklow

ATLANTIC

Killaloe

Nenagh

Barrow

Carlow

Arklow

OCEAN

Kilrush

✈

Thurles

Kilkenny

Limerick

Nore

Shannon

Tipperary

M u n s t e r

Caher

Carrick-on-Suir

Wexford

Rosslare

Tralee

Clonmel

Wexford

St. George's Channel

Dingle

Knockmealdown Mountains

Suir

Waterford

Dingle Bay

Mallow

Blackwater

Dungarvan

Carnsore Point

Killarney

Macgillycuddy's Reeks ▲1041

Boggeragh Mountains

Carrauntoohill

Valencia Island

Cork

Youghal

Kenmare

✈

Cobh

Caha Mountains

Bandon

Bantry

Bantry Bay

Cape Clear

C E L T I C   S E A

West from Greenwich

The Earth as a planet

Relative sizes of the planets

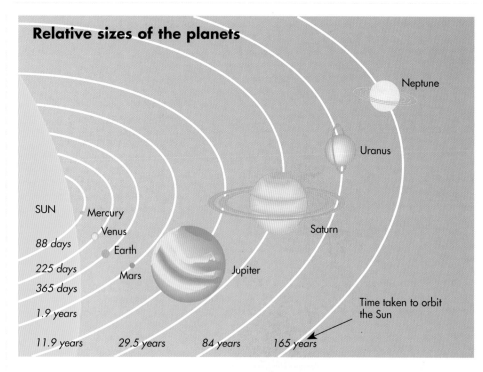

SUN

Mercury
88 days

Venus
225 days

Earth
365 days

Mars
1.9 years

Jupiter
11.9 years

Saturn
29.5 years

Uranus
84 years

Neptune
165 years

Time taken to orbit the Sun

The Solar System

The Earth is one of the eight planets that orbit the Sun. These two diagrams show how big the planets are, how far they are away from the Sun and how long they take to orbit the Sun. The diagram on the left shows how the planets closest to the Sun have the shortest orbits. The Earth takes 365 days (a year) to go round the Sun. The Earth is the fifth largest planet. It is much smaller than Jupiter and Saturn which are the largest planets.

Distances of the planets from the Sun in millions of kilometres

Mercury 58
Venus 108
Earth 150
Mars 228
Asteroids
Jupiter 778
Saturn 1,430
Uranus 2,870
Neptune 4,500

Planet Earth

The Earth spins as if it is on a rod – its axis. The axis would come out of the Earth at two points. The northern point is called the North Pole and the southern point is called the South Pole. The distance between the Poles through the centre of the Earth is 12,700 km.

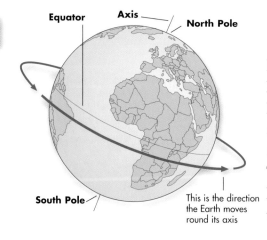

Equator
Axis
North Pole
South Pole
This is the direction the Earth moves round its axis

It takes a day (24 hours) for the Earth to rotate on its axis. It is light (day) when it faces the Sun and dark (night) when it faces away. See the diagram below. The Equator is a line round the Earth which is halfway between the Poles. It is 40,000 km long.

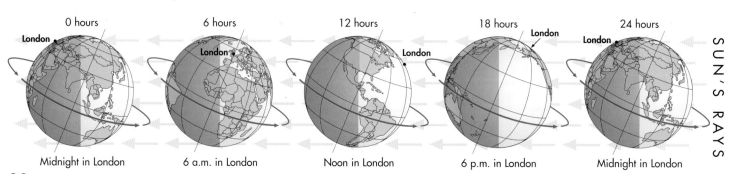

0 hours	6 hours	12 hours	18 hours	24 hours
London	London	London	London	London
Midnight in London	6 a.m. in London	Noon in London	6 p.m. in London	Midnight in London

SUN'S RAYS

28

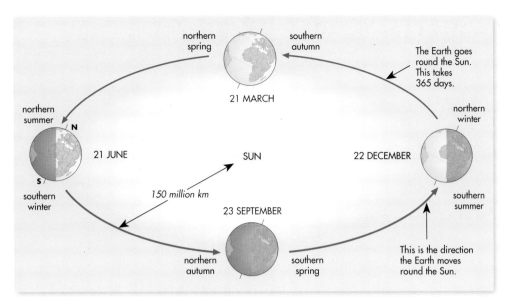

The Earth is always tilted at $66\frac{1}{2}°$. It moves around the Sun. This movement gives us the seasons of the year. In June the northern hemisphere tilts towards the Sun so it is summer. Six months later, in December, the Earth has rotated halfway round the Sun. It is then summer in the southern hemisphere.

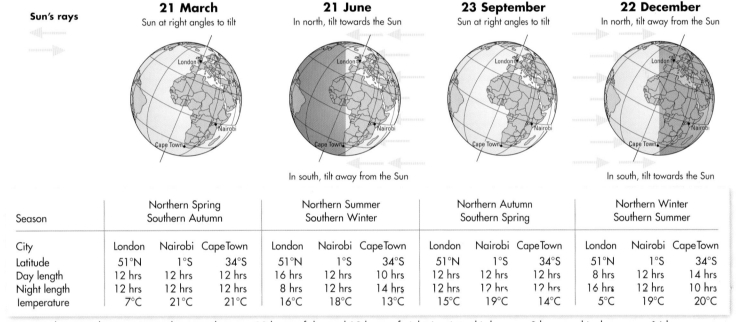

Sun's rays

21 March	**21 June**	**23 September**	**22 December**
Sun at right angles to tilt	In north, tilt towards the Sun	Sun at right angles to tilt	In north, tilt away from the Sun
	In south, tilt away from the Sun		In south, tilt towards the Sun

Season	Northern Spring Southern Autumn			Northern Summer Southern Winter			Northern Autumn Southern Spring			Northern Winter Southern Summer		
City	London	Nairobi	Cape Town	London	Nairobi	Cape Town	London	Nairobi	Cape Town	London	Nairobi	Cape Town
Latitude	51°N	1°S	34°S	51°N	1°S	34°S	51°N	1°S	34°S	51°N	1°S	34°S
Day length	12 hrs	12 hrs	12 hrs	16 hrs	12 hrs	10 hrs	12 hrs	12 hrs	12 hrs	8 hrs	12 hrs	14 hrs
Night length	12 hrs	12 hrs	12 hrs	8 hrs	12 hrs	14 hrs	12 hrs	12 hrs	12 hrs	16 hrs	12 hrs	10 hrs
Temperature	7°C	21°C	21°C	16°C	18°C	13°C	15°C	19°C	14°C	5°C	19°C	20°C

For example, at London in spring and autumn there are 12 hours of day and 12 hours of night. In winter this becomes 8 hours and in the summer 16 hours.

The Moon

The Moon is about a quarter the size of the Earth. It orbits the Earth in just over 27 days (almost a month). The Moon is round but we on Earth see only the parts lit by the Sun. This makes it look as if the Moon is a different shape at different times of the month. These are known as the phases of the Moon and they are shown in this diagram.

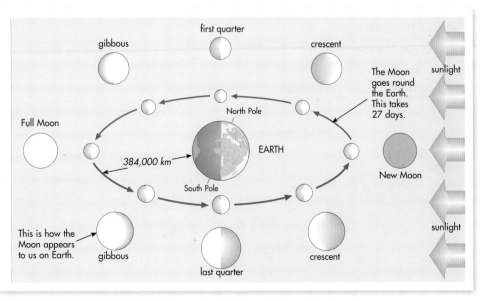

Mountains and rivers

The surface of the Earth is continually being shaped by movements of the Earth's crust. Volcanoes are formed and earthquakes are caused in this way. Rivers also shape the landscape as they flow on their way to the sea.

Volcanoes

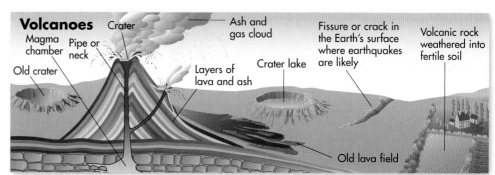

Crater — Ash and gas cloud
Magma chamber
Pipe or neck
Old crater
Layers of lava and ash
Crater lake
Fissure or crack in the Earth's surface where earthquakes are likely
Volcanic rock weathered into fertile soil
Old lava field

The course of a river

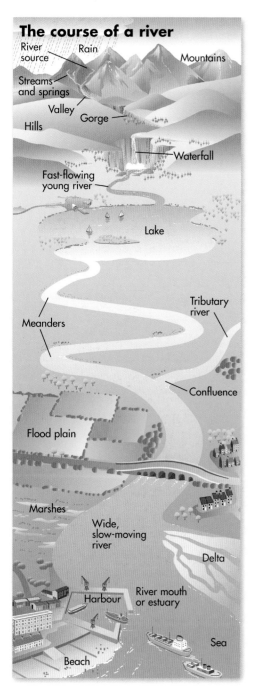

River source
Rain
Mountains
Streams and springs
Valley
Gorge
Hills
Waterfall
Fast-flowing young river
Lake
Meanders
Tributary river
Confluence
Flood plain
Marshes
Wide, slow-moving river
Delta
Harbour
River mouth or estuary
Sea
Beach

Longest rivers	
(kilometres)	
Nile	6,695
Amazon	6,450
Yangtze	6,380

Largest lakes	
(square metres)	
Caspian Sea	371,000
Lake Superior	82,350
Lake Victoria	68,000

Highest mountains	
(metres)	
Everest	8,850
K2	8,611
Kanchenjunga	8,598

Largest islands	
(square kilometres)	
Greenland	2,175,600
New Guinea	821,030
Borneo	744,360

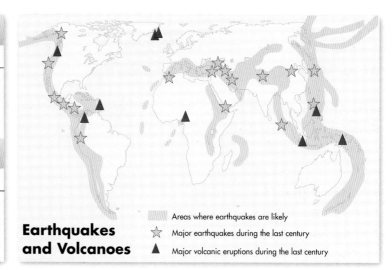

Earthquakes and Volcanoes

- Areas where earthquakes are likely
- ☆ Major earthquakes during the last century
- ▲ Major volcanic eruptions during the last century

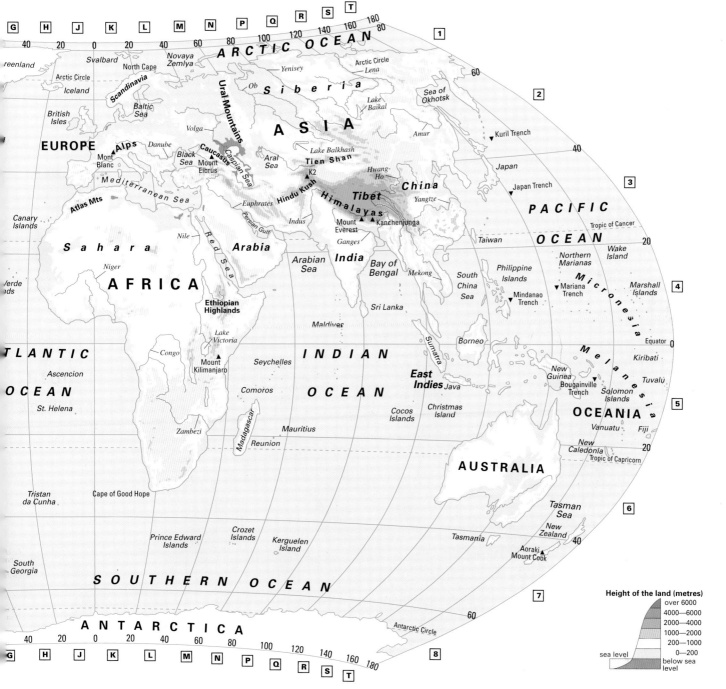

Height of the land (metres)
- over 6000
- 4000—6000
- 2000—4000
- 1000—2000
- 200—1000
- 0—200
- sea level
- below sea level

Climates of the World

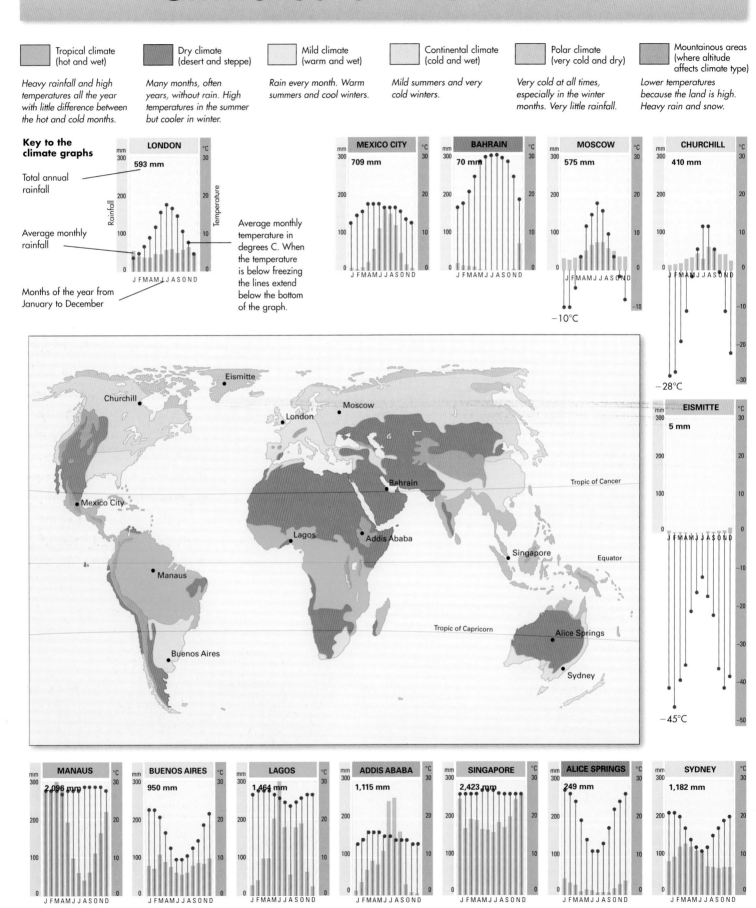

Tropical climate (hot and wet)
Heavy rainfall and high temperatures all the year with little difference between the hot and cold months.

Dry climate (desert and steppe)
Many months, often years, without rain. High temperatures in the summer but cooler in winter.

Mild climate (warm and wet)
Rain every month. Warm summers and cool winters.

Continental climate (cold and wet)
Mild summers and very cold winters.

Polar climate (very cold and dry)
Very cold at all times, especially in the winter months. Very little rainfall.

Mountainous areas (where altitude affects climate type)
Lower temperatures because the land is high. Heavy rain and snow.

Key to the climate graphs

Total annual rainfall

Average monthly rainfall

Months of the year from January to December

Average monthly temperature in degrees C. When the temperature is below freezing the lines extend below the bottom of the graph.

LONDON — 593 mm
MEXICO CITY — 709 mm
BAHRAIN — 70 mm
MOSCOW — 575 mm — −10°C
CHURCHILL — 410 mm — −28°C
EISMITTE — 5 mm — −45°C
MANAUS — 2,096 mm
BUENOS AIRES — 950 mm
LAGOS — 1,464 mm
ADDIS ABABA — 1,115 mm
SINGAPORE — 2,423 mm
ALICE SPRINGS — 249 mm
SYDNEY — 1,182 mm

32

Annual rainfall

Human, plant and animal life cannot live without water. The map on the right shows how much rain falls in different parts of the world. You can see that there is a lot of rain in some places near the Equator. In other places, like the desert areas of the world, there is very little rain. Few plants or animals can survive there. There is also very little rain in the cold lands of the north.

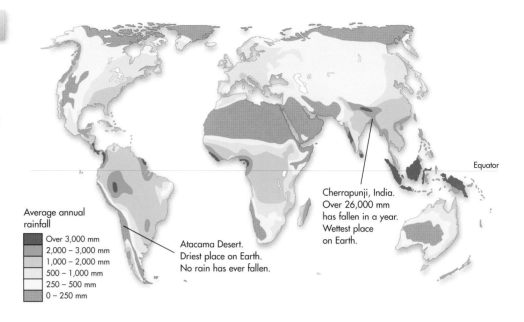

Equator

Average annual rainfall

- Over 3,000 mm
- 2,000 – 3,000 mm
- 1,000 – 2,000 mm
- 500 – 1,000 mm
- 250 – 500 mm
- 0 – 250 mm

Atacama Desert. Driest place on Earth. No rain has ever fallen.

Cherrapunji, India. Over 26,000 mm has fallen in a year. Wettest place on Earth.

Toronto

London

Northern Hemisphere – WINTER

Equator

Tropic of Capricorn

Cape Town

Southern Hemisphere – SUMMER

Adelaide

Buenos Aires

Average temperature in January

- Over 30°C
- 20 – 30°C
- 10 – 20°C
- 0 – 10°C
- −10 – 0°C
- −20 – −10°C
- −30 – −20°C
- −40 – −30°C
- Under −40°C

January temperature

In December, it is winter in the northern hemisphere. It is hot in the southern continents and cold in the northern continents. The North Pole is tilted away from the sun. It is overhead in the regions around the Tropic of Capricorn. This means that there are about 14 hours of daylight in Buenos Aires, Cape Town and Adelaide, and only about 8 hours in London and Toronto.

June temperature

In June, it is summer in the northern hemisphere and winter in the southern hemisphere. It is warmer in the northern lands and colder in the south. The North Pole is tilted towards the sun. This means that in London and Toronto there are about 16 hours of daylight, but in Buenos Aires, Cape Town and Adelaide there are just under 10 hours.

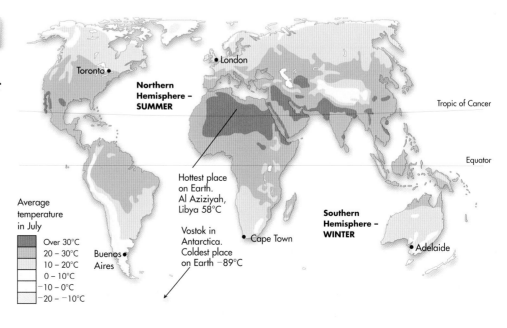

Toronto

London

Northern Hemisphere – SUMMER

Tropic of Cancer

Equator

Hottest place on Earth. Al Aziziyah, Libya 58°C

Vostok in Antarctica. Coldest place on Earth −89°C

Cape Town

Southern Hemisphere – WINTER

Adelaide

Buenos Aires

Average temperature in July

- Over 30°C
- 20 – 30°C
- 10 – 20°C
- 0 – 10°C
- −10 – 0°C
- −20 – −10°C

Forests, grasslands and wastes

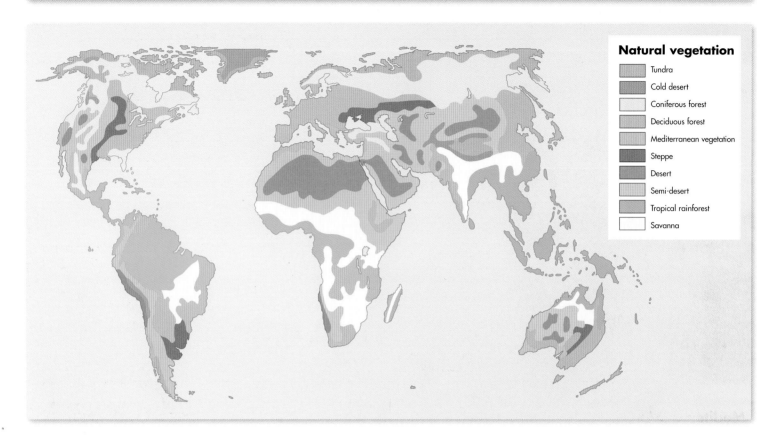

Natural vegetation

- Tundra
- Cold desert
- Coniferous forest
- Deciduous forest
- Mediterranean vegetation
- Steppe
- Desert
- Semi-desert
- Tropical rainforest
- Savanna

The map above shows types of vegetation around the world. The diagram below shows the types of plants which grow on mountains.

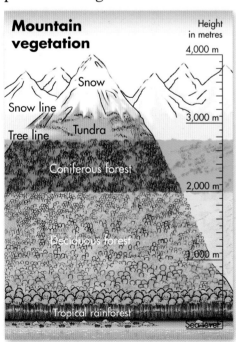

Mountain vegetation

Height in metres

4,000 m

Snow

Snow line

3,000 m

Tree line

Tundra

Coniferous forest

2,000 m

Deciduous forest

1,000 m

Tropical rainforest

Sea level

Tundra

Long, dry, cold winters. Grasses, moss, bog and dwarf trees.

Coniferous forest

Harsh winters, mild summers. Trees have leaves all year.

Mediterranean

Hot, dry summers. Mild wet winters. Plants adapt to the heat.

Desert

Rain is rare. Plants only grow at oases with underground water.

Tropical rainforest (jungle)

Very hot and wet all the year. Tall trees and lush vegetation.

Cold desert

Very cold with little rain or snow. No plants can grow.

Deciduous forest

Rain all year, cool winters. Trees shed leaves in winter.

Steppe

Some rain with a dry season. Grasslands with some trees.

Semi-desert

Poor rains, sparse vegetation. Grass with a few small trees.

Savanna

Mainly dry, but lush grass grows when the rains come.

34

Tundra

Pingo (mound)

Thin, stony soil with permafrost below

Mosses, lichens and herbs

Cold desert

No plants can grow

Coniferous forest

Evergreen conifers (spruces and firs)

Young tree saplings and small shrubs

Carpet of pine needles

Ferns and brambles on edge of forest

Yearly cycle of a deciduous forest

Spring

Summer

Autumn

Winter

Mediterranean

Small stunted trees

Scrub

Steppe

There are many plants in the steppe grasslands.

People planting crops damages the natural habitat.

Tropical rainforest

Scattered trees with umbrella-shaped tops grow the highest.

Main layer of tall trees growing close together.

Creepers grow up the trees to reach the sunlight.

Ferns, mosses and small plants grow closest to the ground.

Desert

Cactus

Sand blown into dunes by the wind

Palm trees

Oasis

Semi-desert

Grass and bush

Joshua trees

Savanna

Dry season

Wet season

Agriculture, forests and fishing

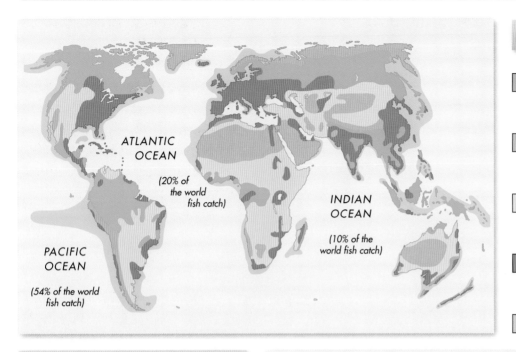

ATLANTIC
OCEAN

(20% of the world fish catch)

INDIAN
OCEAN

(10% of the world fish catch)

PACIFIC
OCEAN

(54% of the world fish catch)

How the land is used

Forest areas with timber. Some hunting and fishing. Agriculture in the tropics.

Deserts and wastelands. Some small areas of agriculture in oases or places that have been irrigated.

Animal farming on large farms (ranches)

Farming of crops and animals on large and small farms

Main fishing areas

The importance of agriculture

Over half the people work in agriculture

Between a quarter and half the people work in agriculture

Between one in ten and a quarter of the people work in agriculture

Less than one in ten of the people work in agriculture

● Countries which depend on agriculture for over half their income

A hundred years ago about 80% of the world's population worked in agriculture. Today it is only about 40% but agriculture is still very important in some countries.

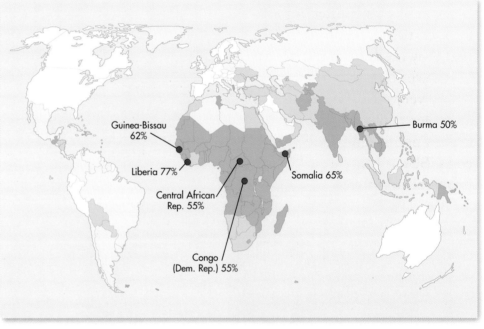

Guinea-Bissau 62%

Liberia 77%

Central African Rep. 55%

Congo (Dem. Rep.) 55%

Somalia 65%

Burma 50%

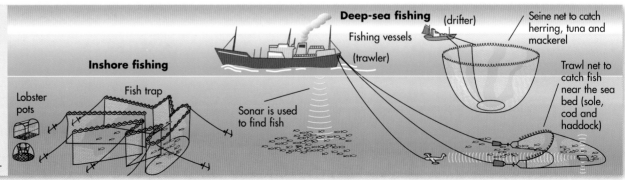

Methods of fishing

There are two types of sea fishing:

1. **Deep-sea fishing** using large trawlers which often stay at sea for many weeks.

2. **Inshore fishing** using small boats, traps and nets up to 70 km from the coast.

Inshore fishing

Lobster pots

Fish trap

Sonar is used to find fish

Deep-sea fishing

(drifter)

Fishing vessels

(trawler)

Seine net to catch herring, tuna and mackerel

Trawl net to catch fish near the sea bed (sole, cod and haddock)

Wheat and rice

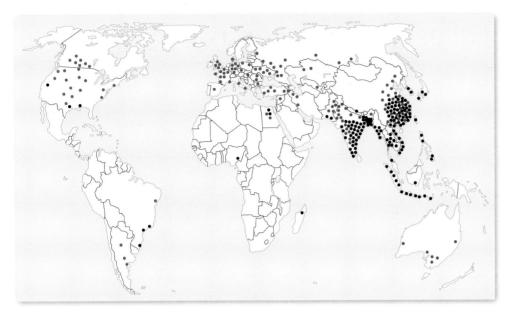

- One dot stands for 4 million tonnes of wheat produced
- One dot stands for 4 million tonnes of rice produced

Wheat is the main cereal crop grown in cooler regions. Rice is the main food for over half the people in the world. It is grown in water in paddy fields in tropical areas. Nearly a third of the world's rice is grown in China.

Cattle and sheep

- One dot stands for 10 million cattle
- One dot stands for 10 million sheep

Meat, milk and leather come from cattle. The map shows that they are kept in most parts of the world except where it is hot or very cold. Sheep are kept in cooler regions and they can live on poorer grassland than cows. Sheep are reared for meat and wool.

Timber

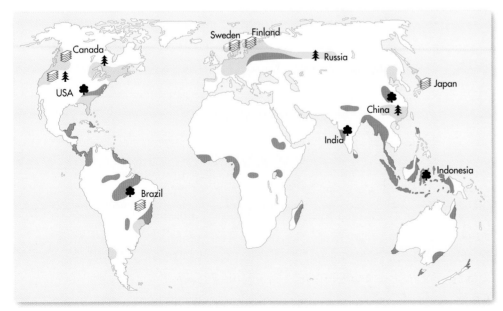

- Main areas where trees are grown for hardwoods (non-coniferous)
- Main areas where trees are grown for softwoods (coniferous)

Countries producing over 5% of
- ♣ the world's hardwood
- ♠ the world's softwood
- the world's wood pulp

Trees are cut down to make timber. Softwood trees such as pines and firs often have cones so they are called coniferous. Some trees are chopped up into wood pulp which is used to make paper.

37

Minerals and energy

Important metals

 Iron ore

△ Bauxite

● Copper

Iron is the most important metal in manufacturing. It is mixed with other metals to make steel which is used for ships, cars and machinery. Bauxite ore is used to make aluminium. Aluminium is light and strong. It is used to make aeroplanes. Copper is used for electric wires, and also to make brass and bronze.

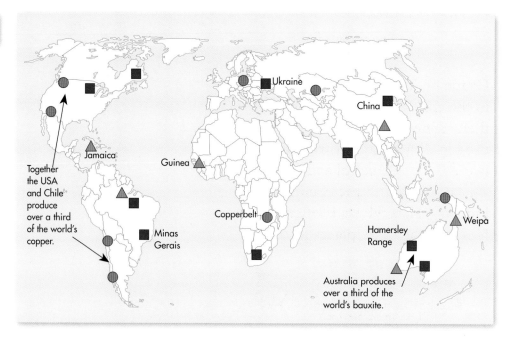

Together the USA and Chile produce over a third of the world's copper.

Ukraine

China

Jamaica

Guinea

Copperbelt

Minas Gerais

Hamersley Range

Weipa

Australia produces over a third of the world's bauxite.

Precious metals and minerals

Gold

☆ Silver

◆ Diamonds

Some minerals like gold, silver and diamonds are used to make jewellery. They are also important in industry. Diamonds are the hardest mineral and so they are used on tools that cut or grind. Silver is used in photography to coat film, and to make electrical goods. Gold is used in the electronics industry.

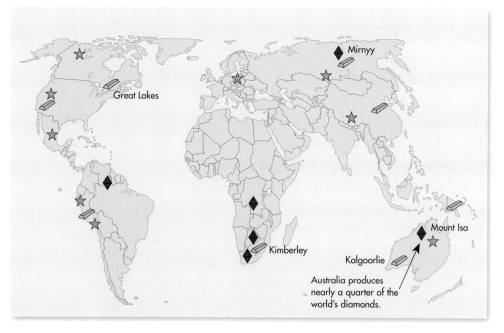

Mirnyy

Great Lakes

Kimberley

Mount Isa

Kalgoorlie

Australia produces nearly a quarter of the world's diamonds.

There are over 70 different types of metals and minerals in the world. The maps above show the main countries where some of the most important ones are mined. After mining, metals and fuels are often exported to other countries where they are manufactured into goods. The map on the left shows which countries depend most on mining for their exports and wealth. These countries are coloured red.

Oil and gas

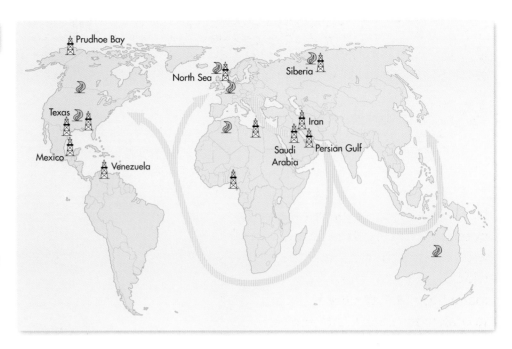

⚒	Oilfields
〜	Natural gasfields
⟹	Main routes for transporting oil and gas by tanker

Crude oil is drilled from deep in the Earth's crust. The oil is then refined so that it can be used in different industries. Oil is used to make petrol and is also very important in the chemical industry. Natural gas is often found in the same places as oil.

Coal

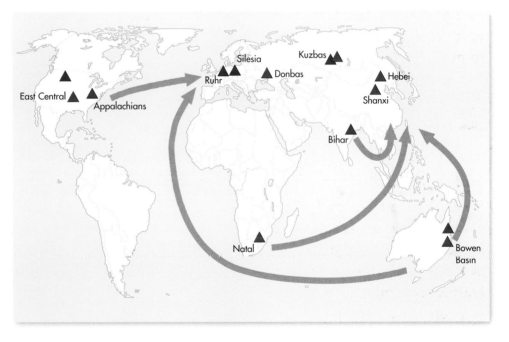

▲	Lignite (soft brown coal)
▲	Hard coal (bituminous)
⟶	Main routes for transporting coal

Coal is a fuel that comes from forests and swamps that rotted millions of years ago and have been crushed by layers of rock. The coal is cut out of the rock from deep mines and also from open-cast mines where the coal is nearer the surface. The oldest type of coal is hard. The coal formed more recently is softer.

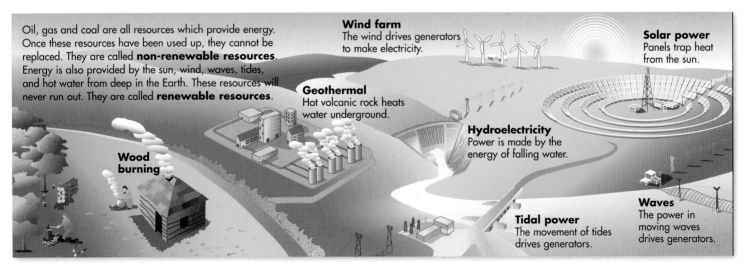

Oil, gas and coal are all resources which provide energy. Once these resources have been used up, they cannot be replaced. They are called **non-renewable resources**. Energy is also provided by the sun, wind, waves, tides, and hot water from deep in the Earth. These resources will never run out. They are called **renewable resources**.

Wind farm
The wind drives generators to make electricity.

Solar power
Panels trap heat from the sun.

Geothermal
Hot volcanic rock heats water underground.

Hydroelectricity
Power is made by the energy of falling water.

Wood burning

Tidal power
The movement of tides drives generators.

Waves
The power in moving waves drives generators.

Peoples and cities of the World

Where people live

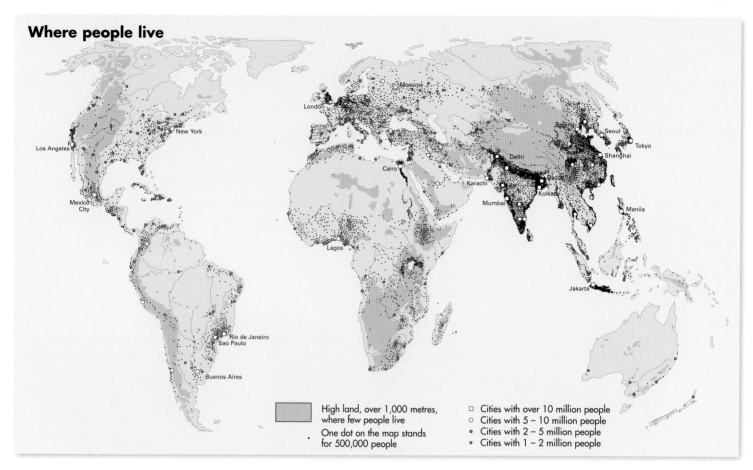

High land, over 1,000 metres, where few people live

One dot on the map stands for 500,000 people

□ Cities with over 10 million people
○ Cities with 5 – 10 million people
• Cities with 2 – 5 million people
• Cities with 1 – 2 million people

The growth of the population of the world 1000–2008 AD

The population of the continents (2006)

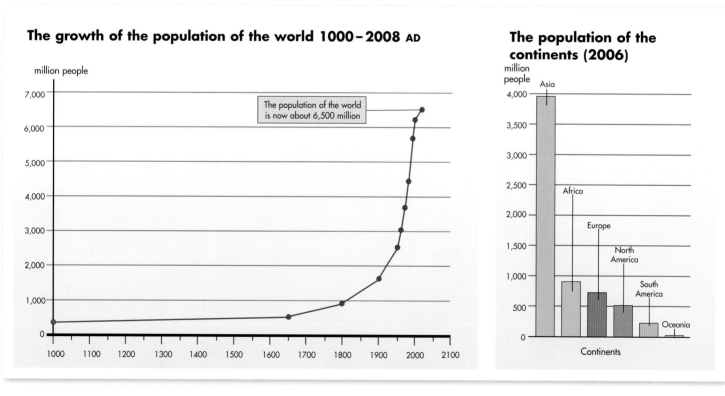

The population of the world is now about 6,500 million

Population by continents

In this diagram the size of each continent is in proportion to its population.

Each square represents 1% of the world population of 6,500 million.

Population of countries in millions

Country	Population
China	1,314
India	1,095
USA	301
Indonesia	245
Brazil	188
Pakistan	166
Bangladesh	147
Russia	143
Nigeria	132
Japan	127
Mexico	107
Philippines	89
Vietnam	84
Germany	82
Egypt	79
Ethiopia	75
Turkey	70
Iran	69
Thailand	65

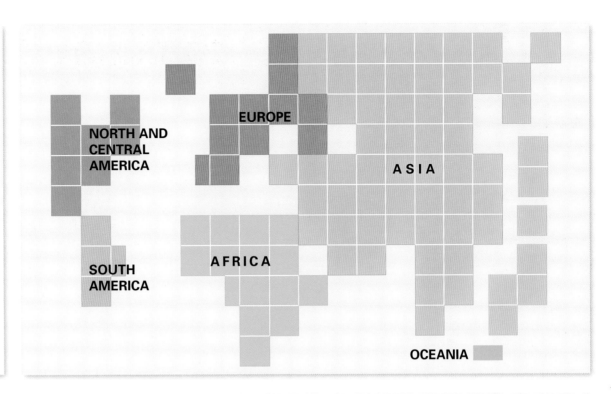

Cities of the World

More people live in cities and towns than in the countryside. These maps show four of the world's largest cities.

Built-up area – houses, shops and factories	Parks and woodland
Poor housing – slums	Favelas – areas of poor housing in Rio de Janeiro
City centre – big shops, offices and government buildings	International airport
	Major roads

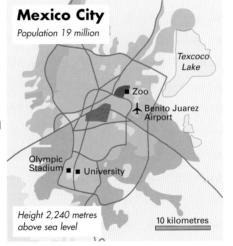

Mexico City
Population 19 million

Texcoco Lake
Zoo
Benito Juarez Airport
Olympic Stadium
University
Height 2,240 metres above sea level
10 kilometres

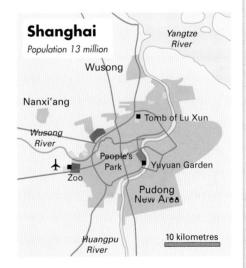

Shanghai
Population 13 million

Yangtze River
Wusong
Nanxi'ang
Tomb of Lu Xun
Wusong River
People's Park
Yuyuan Garden
Zoo
Pudong New Area
Huangpu River
10 kilometres

Rio de Janeiro
Population 11 million

Guanabara Bay
Galeao Airport
Rio Niteroi Bridge
University
Niteroi
Zoo
Maracana Stadium
Corcovado Statue
Sugarloaf Mountain
Copacabana Beach
Ipanema Beach
ATLANTIC OCEAN
10 kilometres

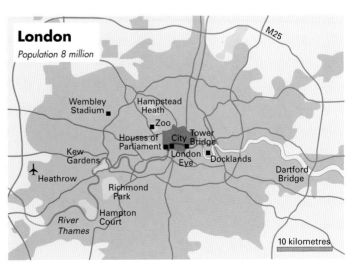

London
Population 8 million

M25
Wembley Stadium
Hampstead Heath
Zoo
Houses of Parliament
City
Tower Bridge
Kew Gardens
London Eye
Docklands
Dartford Bridge
Heathrow
Richmond Park
Hampton Court
River Thames
10 kilometres

Transport and communication

Seaways

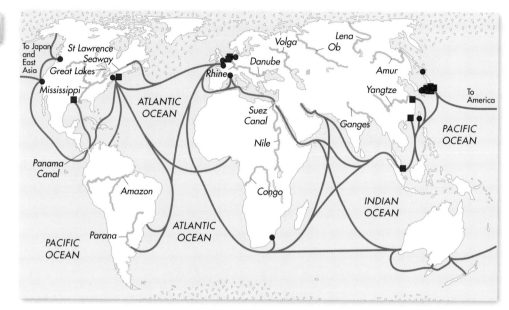

— Main shipping routes

■ The biggest seaports in the world (over a hundred million tonnes of cargo handled a year)

● Other big seaports

▦ Ice and icebergs in the sea all the time, or for some part of the year

— Large ships can sail on these rivers

Sea transport is used for goods that are too bulky or heavy to go by air. The main shipping routes are between North America, Europe and the Far East.

The Panama Canal

Opened in 1914
82 km long
14,000 ships a year

The Suez Canal

Opened in 1870
162 km long
18,000 ships a year

These two important canals cut through narrow pieces of land. Can you work out how much shorter the journeys are by using the canals?

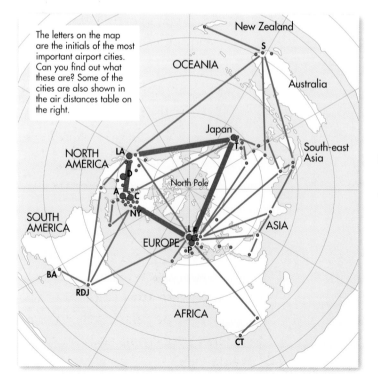

The letters on the map are the initials of the most important airport cities. Can you find out what these are? Some of the cities are also shown in the air distances table on the right.

● Large international airports (over 50 million passengers a year)

· Other important airports

▬ Heavily used air routes

— Other important air routes

Airways

This map has the North Pole at its centre. It shows how much air traffic connects Europe, North America, Japan and Eastern Asia. You can see the long distances in the USA and Russia that are covered by air.

Air distances (kilometres)

	Buenos Aires	Cape Town	London	Los Angeles	New York	Sydney	Tokyo
Buenos Aires		6,880	11,128	9,854	8,526	11,760	18,338
Cape Town	6,880		9,672	16,067	12,551	10,982	14,710
London	11,128	9,672		8,752	5,535	17,005	9,584
Los Angeles	9,854	16,067	8,752		3,968	12,052	8,806
New York	8,526	12,551	5,535	3,968		16,001	10,869
Sydney	11,760	10,982	17,005	12,052	16,001		7,809
Tokyo	18,338	14,710	9,584	8,806	10,869	7,809	

Roads

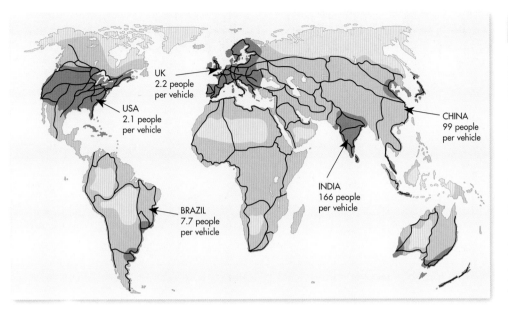

▨	Many roads and motorways
▨	Not many roads, few with hard surfaces and many only tracks. Many roads are through-routes.
▨	No roads or very few roads
—	Important long-distance roads

This map shows some of the major roads that link important cities and ports. It also shows how many people there are in proportion to the number of vehicles in some countries.

Railways

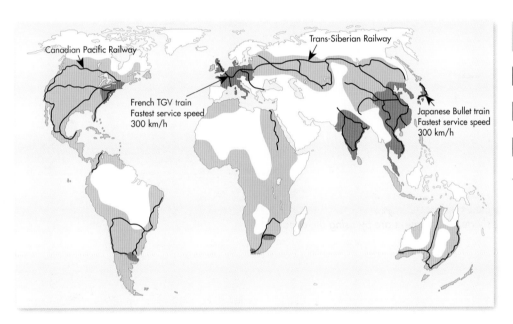

▨	Many passenger and goods lines
▨	Scattered railways often taking goods to and from parts of the coast
▢	No rail services or very few rail services
—	Important long-distance railways

This map shows some of the important long-distance railways in the world. Railways are often used for transporting goods between cities and to ports.

Internet

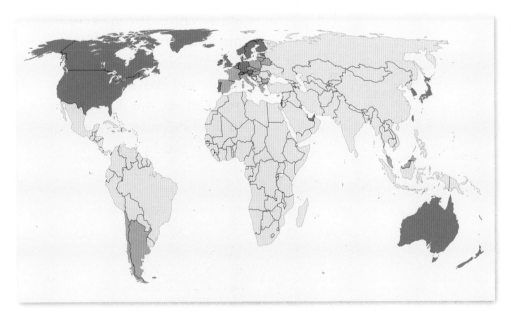

▨	Over half the population use the internet
▨	Between a quarter and a half of the population use the internet
▢	Under a quarter of the population use the internet

The internet started in the 1960s and has now grown into a huge network with over 1.3 billion users around the world. The most popular uses of the internet are email and the world wide web.

Global warming

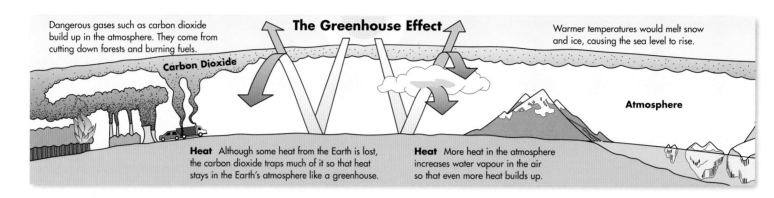

The Greenhouse Effect

Dangerous gases such as carbon dioxide build up in the atmosphere. They come from cutting down forests and burning fuels.

Carbon Dioxide

Warmer temperatures would melt snow and ice, causing the sea level to rise.

Atmosphere

Heat Although some heat from the Earth is lost, the carbon dioxide traps much of it so that heat stays in the Earth's atmosphere like a greenhouse.

Heat More heat in the atmosphere increases water vapour in the air so that even more heat builds up.

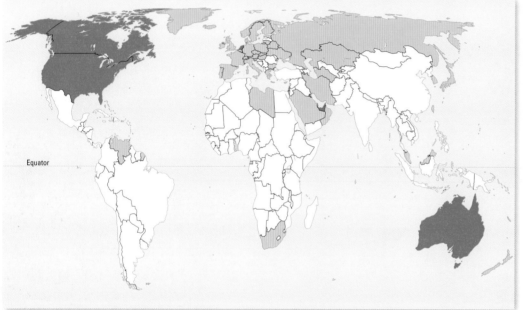

Equator

Carbon dioxide

- ■ Major producers of carbon dioxide
- ■ Other producers of carbon dioxide
- □ Countries producing very little carbon dioxide

This map shows who produces the most carbon dioxide per person. The countries that contribute the most to global warming tend to be rich countries like the USA and Australia. Can you think of reasons why?

Global warming

Experts have studied climate data all around the world. They agreed several years ago that climate change really was happening. Leaders of all the major countries in the world came together in Kyoto in Japan to try and agree on what to do about it. This graph shows how temperatures might not rise as much if countries can cut their carbon dioxide emissions.

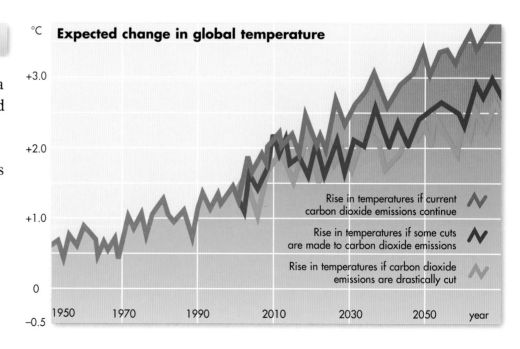

°C **Expected change in global temperature**

+3.0

+2.0

+1.0

Rise in temperatures if current carbon dioxide emissions continue

Rise in temperatures if some cuts are made to carbon dioxide emissions

Rise in temperatures if carbon dioxide emissions are drastically cut

0

1950   1970   1990   2010   2030   2050   year

−0.5

44

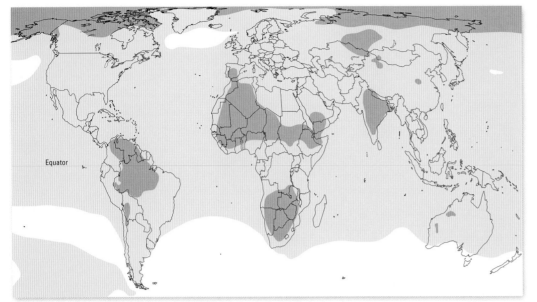

Temperature change

The expected change in temperature in the next 100 years

	More than 5°C warmer
	Betweeen 2°C and 5°C warmer
	Less than 2°C warmer

Compare this map with the map on the opposite page. The countries most affected by temperature change may not be the countries that are causing it.

Rainfall change

The expected change in the amount of rainfall in the next 100 years

	More rainfall
	Very little change in the amount of rainfall
	Less rainfall

As the global climate changes, some parts of the world will get more rainfall, while other parts will become drier. Can you think of the effects this might have?

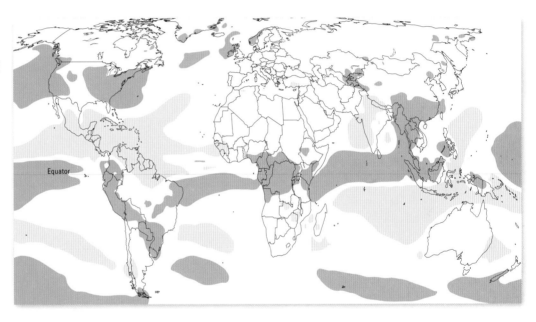

Sea level rise

Areas at risk from rising sea level

Areas with many low-lying islands

Warmer temperatures will result in ice caps melting in Antarctica and Greenland. Sea levels will rise and threaten low-lying coastal areas and islands. Some small islands in the Pacific have already disappeared.

45

Rich and poor

All countries have both rich and poor people but some countries have more poor people than others. The amount of food that people have to eat and the age that they die can often depend on where they live in the world. The world can be divided into two parts – the rich and the poor.

The richer countries are mostly in the North and the poorer countries are mostly in the South. The map below shows which countries are rich and which are poor. The list on the right shows some contrasts between rich and poor. Some of these contrasts can be seen in the maps on these pages.

Rich	**Poor**
Healthy	Poor health
Educated	Poor education
Well fed	Poorly fed
Small families	Large families
Many industries	Few industries
Few farmers	Many farmers
Give aid	Receive aid

The South has over three-quarters of the world's population but less than a quarter of its wealth.

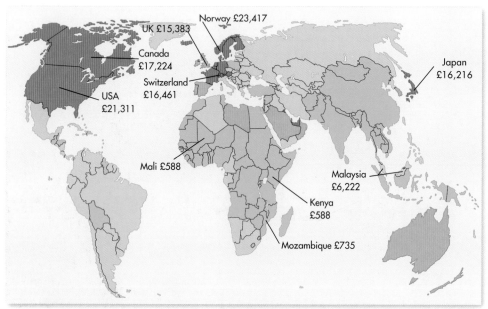

Income

- Very rich countries
- Rich countries
- Poor countries
- Very poor countries

The map shows how much money there is to spend on each person in a country. This is called income per person – this is worked out by dividing the wealth of a country by its population. The map gives examples of rich and poor countries.

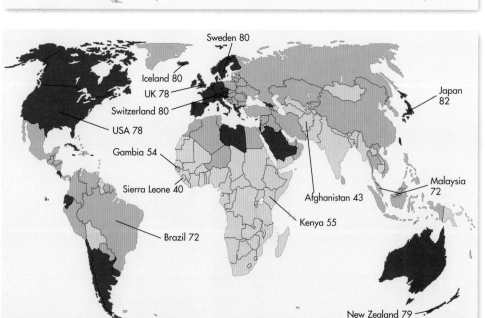

How long do people live?

This is the average age when people die

- Over 75 years
- 60 – 75 years
- Under 60 years

The average age of death is called life expectancy. In the world as a whole, the average life expectancy is 65 years. Some of the highest and lowest ages of death are shown on the map.

Food and famine

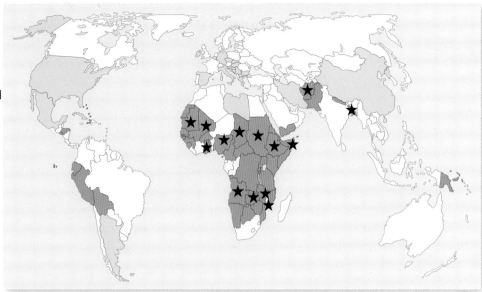

If people do not have enough to eat they become unhealthy. This map shows where in the world people have less than and more than the amount of food they need to live a healthy life.

Reading and writing

The map shows the proportion of adults in each country who cannot read or write a simple sentence. Can you think of some reasons why more people cannot read or write in some places in the world than in others?

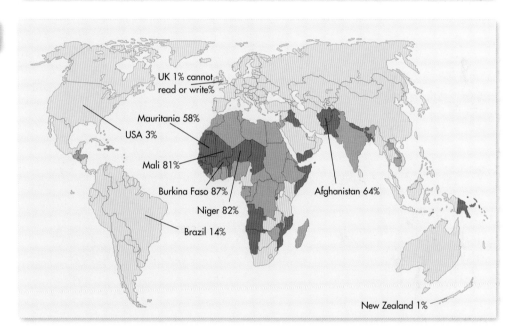

UK 1% cannot read or write%
Mauritania 58%
USA 3%
Mali 81%
Burkina Faso 87%
Niger 82%
Brazil 14%
Afghanistan 64%
New Zealand 1%

Development aid

Some countries receive aid from other countries. Money is one type of aid. It is used to help with food, health and education problems. The map shows how much different countries give or receive.

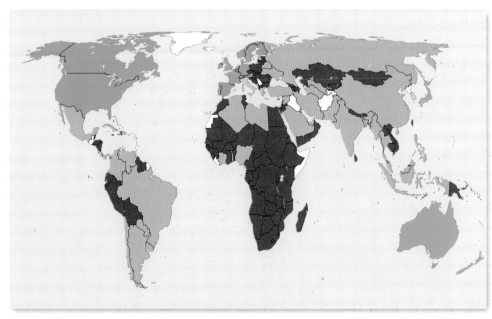

Countries of the World

North America

(see pages 58–59)

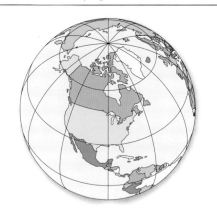

These pages show different maps of the world. The large map shows the world cut through the Pacific Ocean and opened out on to flat paper. The smaller maps of the continents are views of the globe looking down on each of the continents.

Larger maps of the continents appear on the following pages. They show more cities than on this map

South America

(see pages 60–61)

Africa

(see pages 54–55)

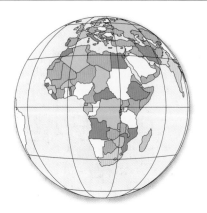

■ Cities with more than 10 million people

48

Europe
(see pages 50–51)

Asia
(see pages 52–53)

Oceania
(see pages 56–57)

EENLAND
(Denmark)

Svalbard
(Norway)

Arctic Circle

ICELAND

NORWAY SWEDEN FINLAND

UNITED
KINGDOM DENMARK

IRELAND

ESTONIA
LATVIA
LITHUANIA
BELARUS

Moscow

R U S S I A

60

NETH.
GERMANY POLAND
BELG. LUX. CZECH. SLOV.
AUSTRIA HUNG.
FRANCE SWITZ. SLO.
CR.
B.-H.
ITALY
ALB. MAC.

UKRAINE
MOLDOVA

ROMANIA

BULGARIA

KAZAKHSTAN

MONGOLIA

40

PORTUGAL SPAIN

GREECE

TURKEY

GEORGIA
ARM. AZER.

UZBEKISTAN

KYRGYZSTAN

Beijing

NORTH
KOREA

JAPAN

CYPRUS
LEB.

SYRIA

TURKMENISTAN

TAJIKISTAN

Seoul
SOUTH
KOREA

Tokyo

C H I N A

ISRAEL
JORDAN

IRAQ

IRAN

AFGHANISTAN

Shanghai

P A C I F I C

MOROCCO

Cairo

KUWAIT

PAKISTAN

Delhi

NEPAL BHUTAN

Tropic of Cancer

Canary Islands
(Spain)

ALGERIA

LIBYA

EGYPT

BAHRAIN QATAR
U.A.E.

Karachi

BANGLA-
DESH

TAIWAN

20

ores
rtugal)

WESTERN
SAHARA

SAUDI
ARABIA

OMAN

Kolkata

Mumbai

Dacca

BURMA
(Myanmar)

O C E A N

N

MAURITANIA

MALI

NIGER

CHAD

SUDAN

ERITREA

YEMEN

INDIA

LAOS
THAI-
LAND

Manila

PHILIPPINES

Guam
(U.S.A.)

NORTHERN
MARIANAS

PE
RDE
NDS

SENEGAL

BURKINA
FASO

DJIBOUTI

SRI
LANKA

Bangkok

CAMBODIA

VIETNAM

MARSHALL
ISLANDS

GAMBIA
GUINEA-
BISSAU

GUINEA

NIGERIA

CENTRAL
AFRICAN
REP.

ETHIOPIA

SOMALI
REP.

MALDIVES

BRUNEI

PALAU

FEDERATED STATES
OF MICRONESIA

SIERRA
LEONE

IVORY
COAST

GHANA

Lagos

CAMEROON

MALAYSIA

LIBERIA

EQUATORIAL
GUINEA

GABON

Democratic
Republic
of the
CONGO

UGANDA

KENYA

SEYCHELLES

SINGAPORE

I N D O N E S I A

New
Guinea

PAPUA
NEW
GUINEA

Equator

SOLOMON
ISLANDS

KIRIBATI

Ascencion
(U.K.)

CONGO

CABINDA

RWANDA
BURUNDI

TANZANIA

I N D I A N

Borneo

Sumatra

Jakarta

EAST
TIMOR

TUVALU

St. Helena
(U.K.)

ANGOLA

MALAWI

ZAMBIA

COMOROS

O C E A N

Cocos Islands
(Australia)

Christmas
Island
(Australia)

VANUATU

FIJI

S O U T H

ZIMBABWE

MOZAMBIQUE

MADAGASCAR

MAURITIUS

NAMIBIA

BOTSWANA

R union
(France)

New
Caledonia
(France)

Tropic of Capricorn

20

SWAZILAND

T L A N T I C

SOUTH
AFRICA

LESOTHO

A U S T R A L I A

Tristan da
Cunha (U.K.)

O C E A N

Prince Edward
Islands
(South Africa)

Crozet Islands
(France)

NEW
ZEALAND

40

South Georgia
(U.K.)

Kerguelen Islands
(France)

S O U T H E R N   O C E A N

A n t a r c t i c a

60

Antarctic Circle

West from Greenwich   East from Greenwich

ALB.	= Albania	LEB.	= Lebanon
ARM.	= Armenia	LUX.	= Luxembourg
AZER.	= Azerbaijan	MAC.	= Macedonia
BELG.	= Belgium	M.	= Montenegro
B.-H.	= Bosnia-Herzegovina	NETH.	= Netherlands
CR.	= Croatia	S.	= Serbia
CZECH.	= Czech Republic	SLOV.	= Slovenia
DOM. REP.	= Dominican Republic	SWITZ.	= Switzerland
HUNG.	= Hungary	U.A.E.	= United Arab Emirates
K.	= Kosovo		

Europe

Largest countries – by area

(thousand square kilometres)

Russia	17,075
Ukraine	604
France	552
Spain	498

Largest countries – by population

(million people)

Russia	143
Germany	82
France	61
United Kingdom	61

Largest cities

(million people)

Moscow (RUSSIA)	10.7
Paris (FRANCE)	9.6
Istanbul (TURKEY)	9.0
London (UK)	9.0

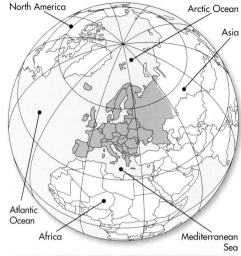

- *Europe is the second smallest continent. It is one fifth the size of Asia. Australia is slightly smaller than Europe.*
- *Great Britain is the largest island in Europe.*
- *Some people think that the whole of Turkey and Cyprus should be included in Europe.*

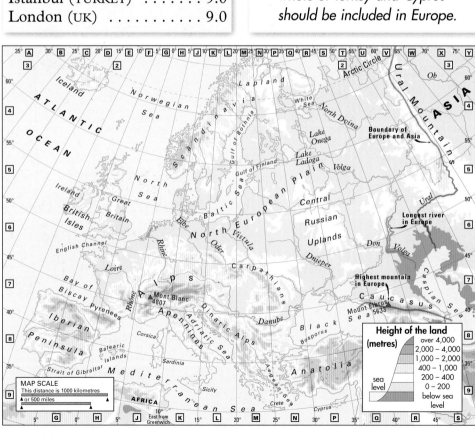

Height of the land
(metres)
over 4,000
2,000 – 4,000
1,000 – 2,000
400 – 1,000
200 – 400
0 – 200
below sea level

MAP SCALE
This distance is 1000 kilometres
or 500 miles

Asia

Largest countries – by area
(thousand square kilometres)

Russia	17,075
China	9,597
India	3,287

Largest countries – by population
(million people)

China	1,314
India	1,095
Indonesia	245
Russia	143

Largest cities
(million people)

Mumbai (INDIA)	18.3
Delhi (INDIA)	15.3
Kolkata (INDIA)	14.3
Shanghai (CHINA)	12.7
Dacca (BANGLADESH)	12.6

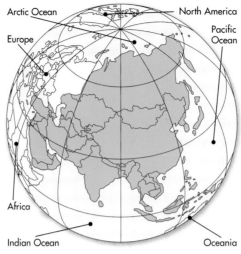

■ *Asia is the largest continent. It is twice the size of North America.*
■ *It is a continent of long rivers. Many of Asia's rivers are longer than Europe's longest rivers.*
■ *Asia contains well over half the world's population.*

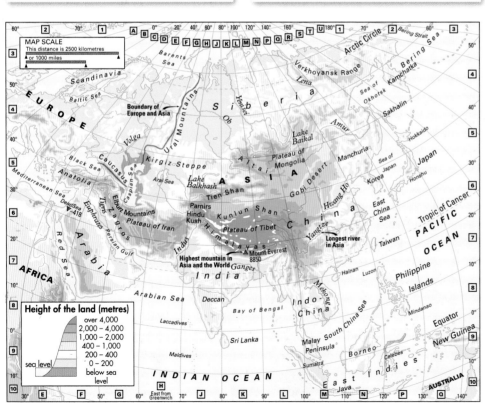

Height of the land (metres)
- over 4,000
- 2,000 – 4,000
- 1,000 – 2,000
- 400 – 1,000
- 200 – 400
- 0 – 200
- below sea level
- sea level

Map information

■● Cities	—— Country boundary
★ Capital city	☐ Sea and lakes
Ⓐ Index square – see index	

MAP SCALE
This distance is 2000 kilometres
or 1000 miles

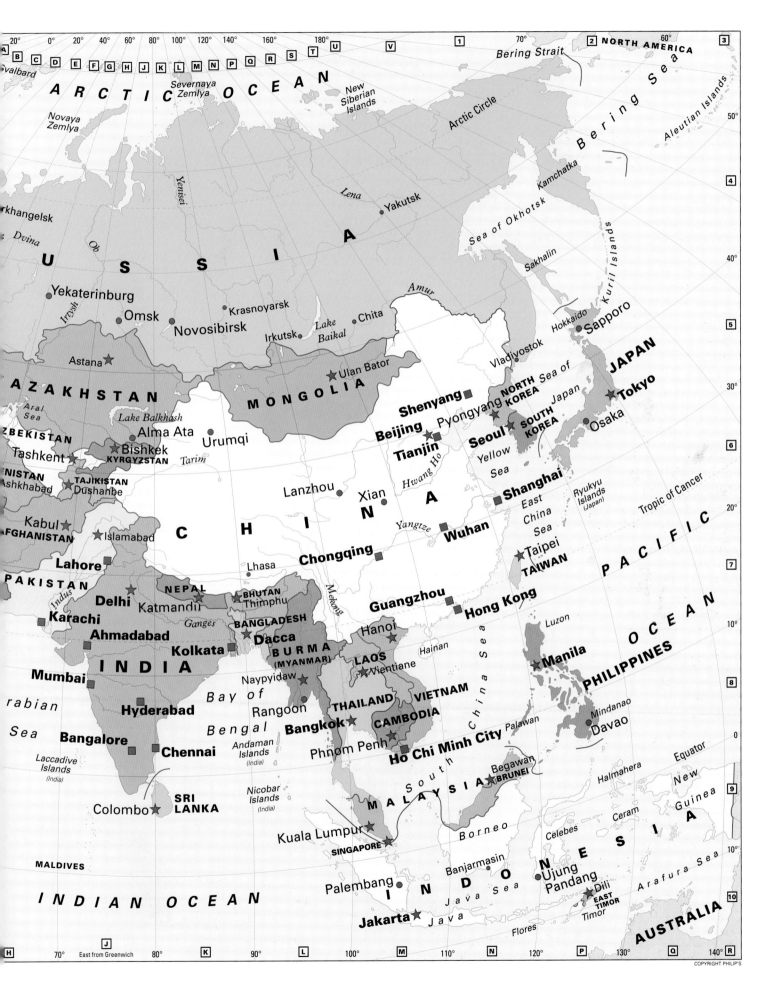

Africa

- Africa is the second largest continent. Asia is the largest.
- There are over 50 countries, some of them small in area and population. The population of Africa is growing more quickly than any other continent.
- Parts of Africa have a dry, desert climate. Other parts are tropical.

- The highest mountains run from north to south on the eastern side of Africa. The Great Rift Valley is a volcanic valley that was formed 10 to 20 million years ago by a crack in the Earth's crust. Mount Kenya and Mount Kilimanjaro are examples of old volcanoes in the area.
- The Sahara desert is the largest desert in the world.

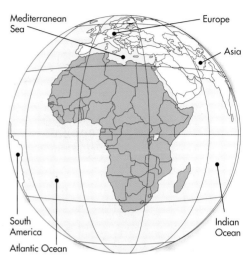

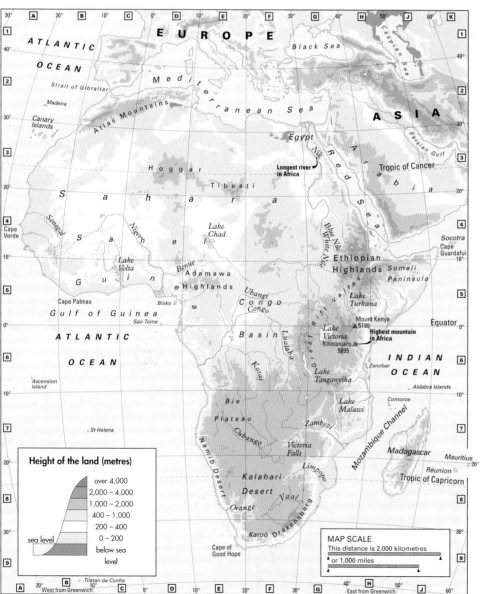

Largest countries – by area

(thousand square kilometres)

Sudan	2,506
Algeria	2,382
Congo (Dem. Rep.)	2,345
Libya	1,760
Chad	1,284
Niger	1,267

Largest countries – by population

(million people)

Nigeria	132
Egypt	79
Ethiopia	75
Congo (Dem. Rep.)	63
South Africa	44
Tanzania	37

Largest cities

(million people)

Cairo (EGYPT)	11.1
Lagos (NIGERIA)	11.1
Kinshasa (CONGO, DEM. REP.)	5.7
Alexandria (EGYPT)	3.8
Casablanca (MOROCCO)	3.7

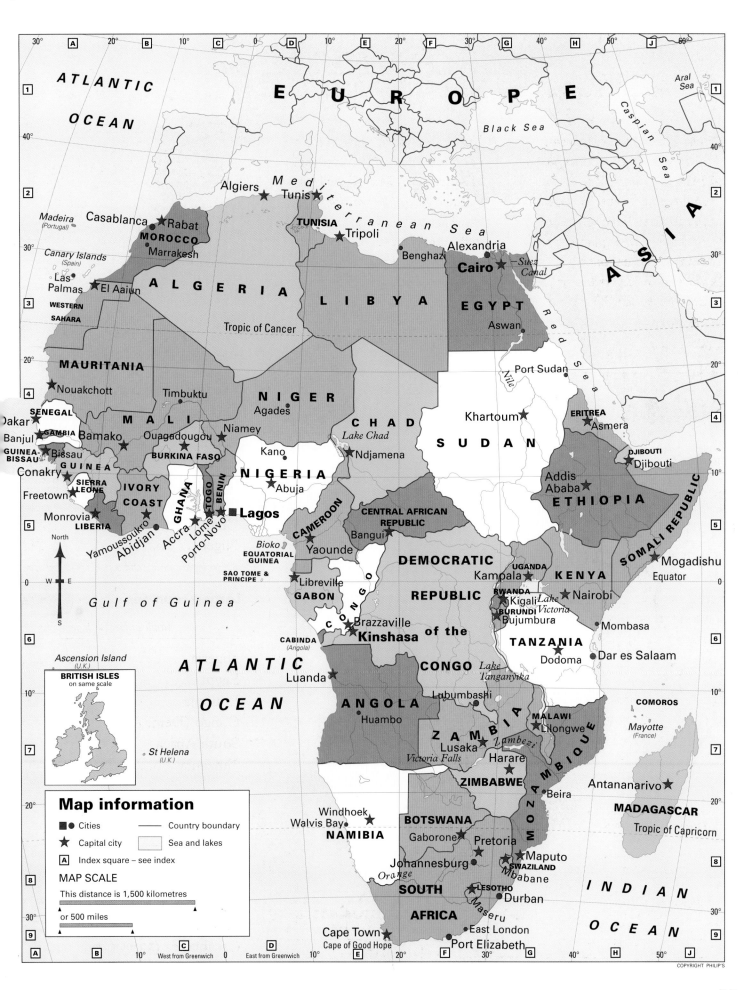

ATLANTIC
OCEAN

EUROPE

Aral Sea

ASIA

Black Sea

Caspian Sea

Mediterranean Sea

Algiers ★ Tunis ★
TUNISIA
Casablanca ● ★ Rabat Tripoli ★
MOROCCO
Benghazi ● Alexandria ●
Marrakesh ● **Cairo** ★ — *Suez Canal*

Madeira (Portugal)
Canary Islands (Spain)
Las ● Palmas
El Aaiun ● **ALGERIA** **LIBYA** **EGYPT**
WESTERN SAHARA Aswan ●

Tropic of Cancer

Red Sea

Nile

MAURITANIA
Nouakchott ★ Timbuktu ● **NIGER** **CHAD** Khartoum ★ Port Sudan ●
SENEGAL Agades ● **ERITREA**
Dakar ★ **MALI** Niamey ★ *Lake Chad* **SUDAN** Asmera ★
Banjul ★ Bamako ★ Ouagadougou ★ Kano ● Ndjamena ★ **DJIBOUTI** ★
GAMBIA **BURKINA FASO** Djibouti ●
GUINEA-BISSAU Bissau ★ **NIGERIA** Addis **ETHIOPIA**
GUINEA **GHANA** **TOGO** **BENIN** Abuja ★ Ababa ★
Conakry ★ **SIERRA LEONE** **IVORY COAST** **CENTRAL AFRICAN REPUBLIC** **SOMALI REPUBLIC**
Freetown ★ Lagos ■ Bangui ★
Monrovia ★ Yamoussoukro ● Accra ★ Lome ★ Porto-Novo ★ **CAMEROON** **DEMOCRATIC** Mogadishu ●
LIBERIA Abidjan ● Yaounde ★ **UGANDA** **KENYA** Equator
Bioko **REPUBLIC** Kampala ★
North **EQUATORIAL GUINEA** **RWANDA** Nairobi ★
SAO TOME & PRINCIPE Libreville ★ Kigali ★ *Lake Victoria*
W ─ E **GABON** **CONGO** **BURUNDI** Mombasa ●
S Brazzaville ★ Bujumbura ★
0 *Gulf of Guinea* **Kinshasa** **of the** **TANZANIA**
CABINDA (Angola) Dodoma ★ Dar es Salaam ●

ATLANTIC **CONGO** *Lake Tanganyika*
OCEAN Luanda ★
Lubumbashi ● **COMOROS**
ANGOLA **MALAWI** *Mayotte (France)*
Huambo ● Lilongwe ★
ZAMBIA *Zambezi*
Lusaka ★ **MOZAMBIQUE**
Victoria Falls Harare ★ Antananarivo ★
ZIMBABWE Beira ●
Windhoek ★ **MADAGASCAR**
Walvis Bay ● **BOTSWANA** Tropic of Capricorn
NAMIBIA Gaborone ★ Pretoria ★
Johannesburg ● Maputo ★
SWAZILAND
Orange Mbabane ★
LESOTHO
SOUTH Maseru ★ Durban ●
AFRICA *Maseru* East London ●
Cape Town ★ Port Elizabeth ●
Cape of Good Hope

INDIAN

OCEAN

Ascension Island (U.K.)

BRITISH ISLES on same scale

St Helena (U.K.)

Map information

- ■ ● Cities
- ★ Capital city
- Ⓐ Index square – see index
- —— Country boundary
- ▭ Sea and lakes

MAP SCALE

This distance is 1,500 kilometres

or 500 miles

West from Greenwich East from Greenwich

COPYRIGHT PHILIP'S

55

Australia and Oceania

- *The continent is often called Oceania. It is made up of the huge island of Australia and thousands of other islands in the Pacific Ocean.*
- *It is the smallest continent, only about a sixth the size of Asia.*
- *The highest mountain is on the Indonesian part of New Guinea which many consider to be part of Asia.*

Largest countries – by area

(thousand square kilometres)

Australia	7,741
Papua New Guinea	463
New Zealand	271

Largest countries – by population

(million people)

Australia	20
Papua New Guinea	6

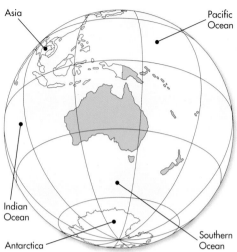

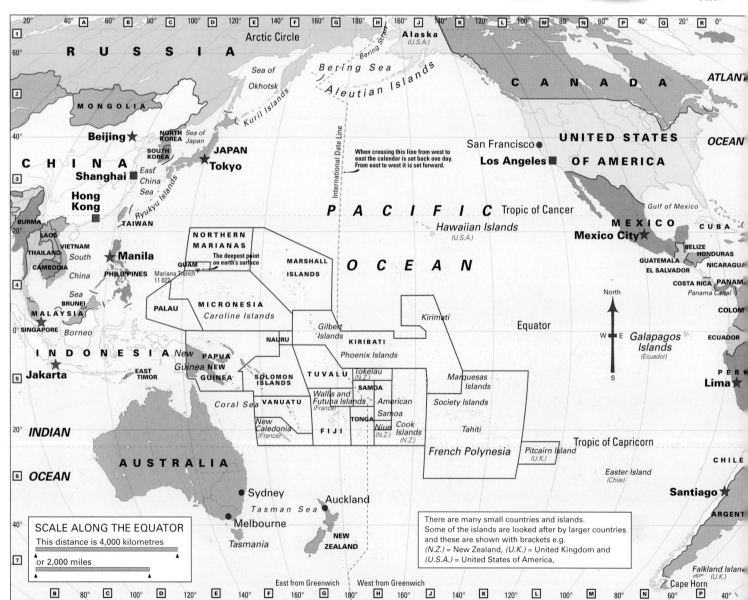

When crossing this line from west to east the calendar is set back one day. From east to west it is set forward.

SCALE ALONG THE EQUATOR

This distance is 4,000 kilometres

or 2,000 miles

There are many small countries and islands. Some of the islands are looked after by larger countries and these are shown with brackets e.g. (N.Z.) = New Zealand, (U.K.) = United Kingdom and (U.S.A.) = United States of America,

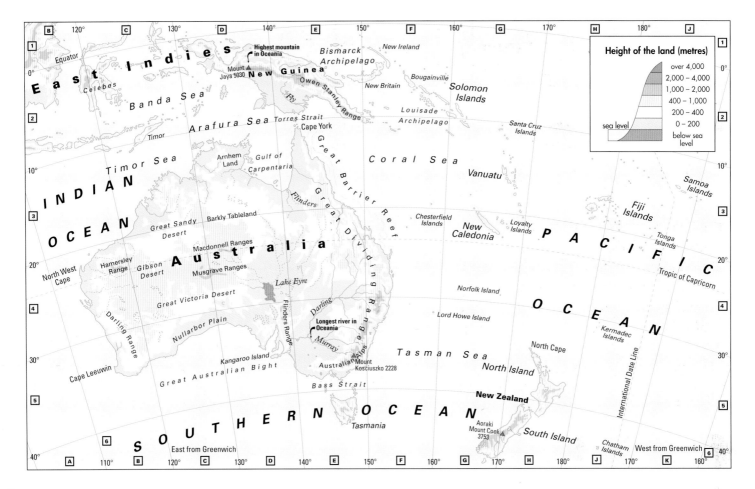

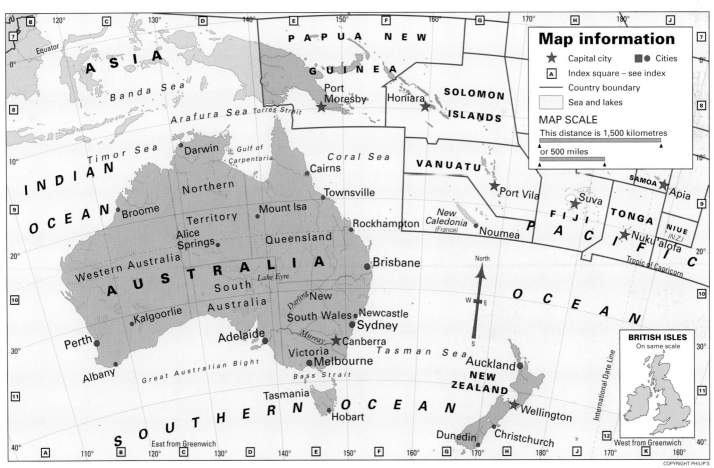

North America

- North America is the third largest continent. It is half the size of Asia. It stretches almost from the Equator to the North Pole.
- Three countries – Canada, the United States and Mexico – make up most of the continent.
- Greenland, the largest island in the world, is included within North America.

- In the east there are a series of large lakes. These are called the Great Lakes. A large waterfall called Niagara Falls is between Lake Erie and Lake Ontario. The St Lawrence river connects the Great Lakes with the Atlantic Ocean.
- North and South America are joined by a narrow strip of land called the Isthmus of Panama.

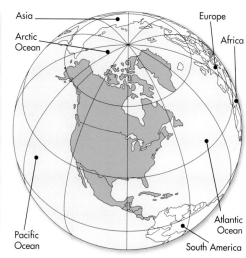

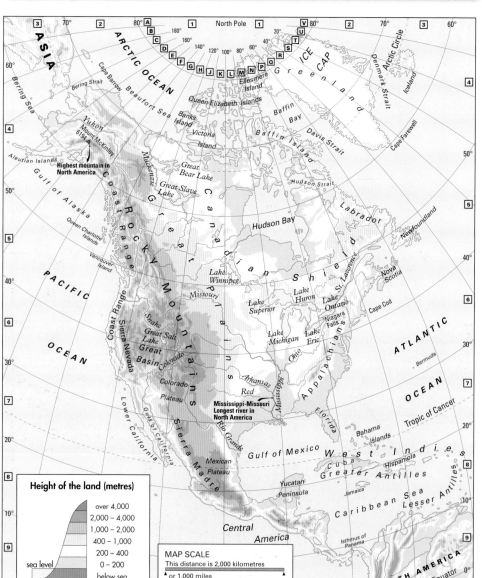

Largest countries – by area

(thousand square kilometres)

Canada	9,971
United States	9,629
Greenland	2,176
Mexico	1,958
Nicaragua	130
Honduras	112

Largest countries – by population

(million people)

United States	301
Mexico	107
Canada	33
Guatemala	12
Cuba	11
Dominican Republic	9

Largest cities

(million people)

Mexico City (MEXICO)	19.0
New York (USA)	17.8
Los Angeles (USA)	11.8
Chicago (USA)	8.3
Philadelphia (USA)	5.1

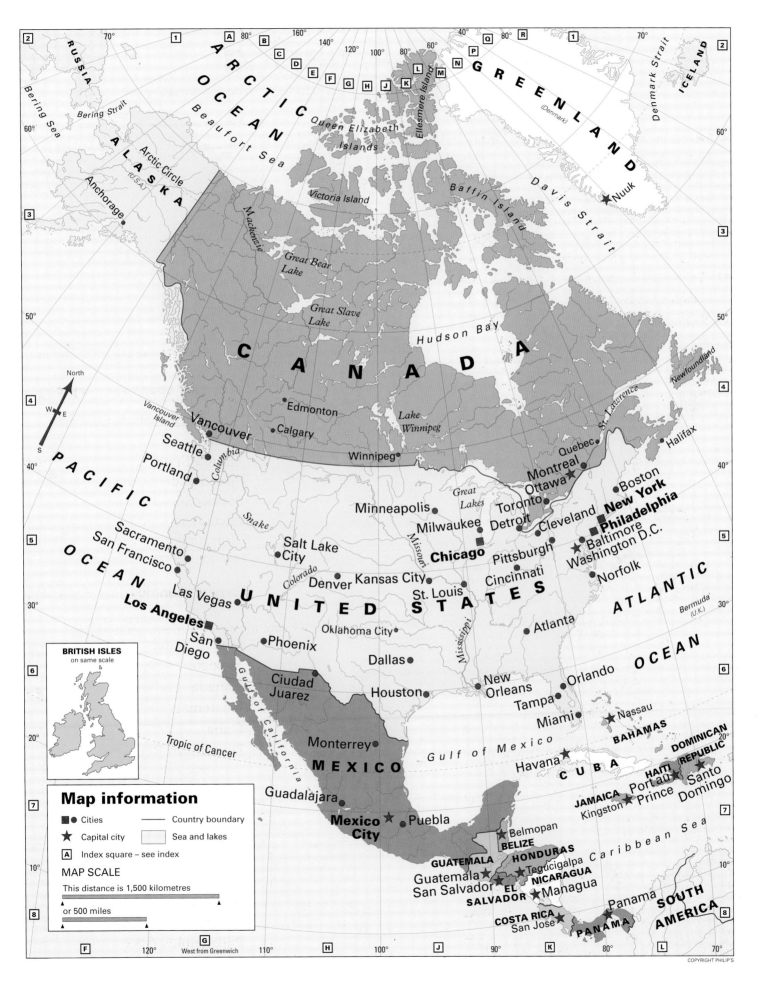

RUSSIA

ARCTIC OCEAN

Bering Sea

Bering Strait

Beaufort Sea

ALASKA (U.S.A.)

Arctic Circle

Anchorage

Mackenzie

GREENLAND (Denmark)

Denmark Strait

ICELAND

Queen Elizabeth Islands

Ellesmere Island

Victoria Island

Baffin Island

Davis Strait

Nuuk

Great Bear Lake

Great Slave Lake

Hudson Bay

C A N A D A

Newfoundland

North

W E

S

PACIFIC OCEAN

Vancouver Island

Vancouver

Seattle

Portland

Columbia

Edmonton

Calgary

Lake Winnipeg

Winnipeg

St. Lawrence

Quebec

Montreal

Ottawa

Halifax

Sacramento

San Francisco

Las Vegas

Los Angeles

San Diego

Snake

Salt Lake City

Denver

Colorado

Phoenix

Minneapolis

Milwaukee

Missouri

Chicago

Kansas City

St. Louis

Oklahoma City

Dallas

Great Lakes

Toronto

Detroit

Cleveland

Pittsburgh

Cincinnati

U N I T E D   S T A T E S

Atlanta

New York

Philadelphia

Baltimore

Washington D.C.

Norfolk

Boston

ATLANTIC

Bermuda (U.K.)

OCEAN

Mississippi

Houston

New Orleans

Tampa

Miami

Orlando

Gulf of Mexico

Havana

CUBA

Nassau

BAHAMAS

DOMINICAN REPUBLIC

HAITI

Port au Prince

Santo Domingo

JAMAICA

Kingston

Ciudad Juarez

Gulf of California

Monterrey

MEXICO

Guadalajara

Mexico City

Puebla

Tropic of Cancer

BELIZE

Belmopan

GUATEMALA

Guatemala

San Salvador

EL SALVADOR

HONDURAS

Tegucigalpa

NICARAGUA

Managua

COSTA RICA

San Jose

Caribbean Sea

Panama

PANAMA

SOUTH AMERICA

BRITISH ISLES
on same scale

Map information

■● Cities

★ Capital city

Ⓐ Index square – see index

— Country boundary

Sea and lakes

MAP SCALE

This distance is 1,500 kilometres

or 500 miles

West from Greenwich

COPYRIGHT PHILIP'S

59

South America

- The Amazon is the second longest river in the world. The Nile is the longest river, but more water flows from the Amazon into the ocean than from any other river.
- The range of mountains called the Andes runs for over 7,500 km from north to south on the western side of the continent. There are many volcanoes in the Andes.

- Lake Titicaca is the largest lake in the continent. It has an area of 8,300 sq km and is 3,800 metres above sea level.
- Spanish and Portuguese are the principal languages spoken in South America.
- Brazil is the largest country in area and population and is the richest in the continent.

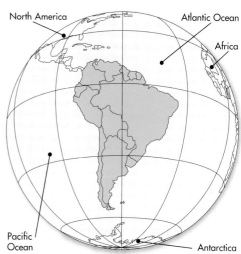

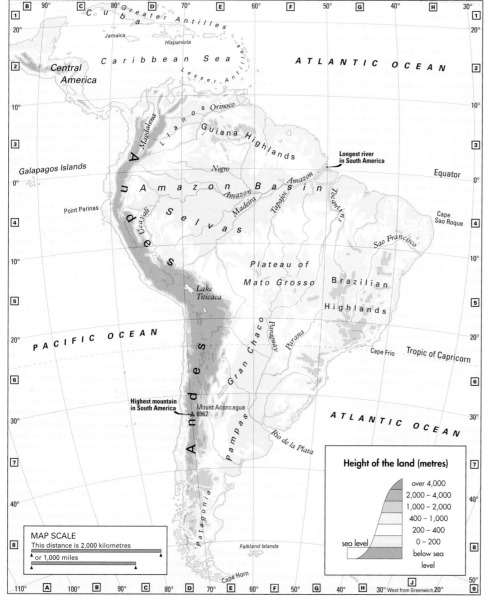

Largest countries – by area

(thousand square kilometres)

Brazil	8,514
Argentina	2,780
Peru	1,285
Colombia	1,139
Bolivia	1,099
Venezuela	912

Largest countries – by population

(million people)

Brazil	188
Colombia	44
Argentina	40
Peru	28
Venezuela	26
Chile	16

Largest cities

(million people)

Sao Paulo (BRAZIL)	18.0
Buenos Aires (ARGENTINA)	13.3
Rio de Janeiro (BRAZIL)	11.5
Lima (PERU)	8.2
Bogota (COLOMBIA)	7.6

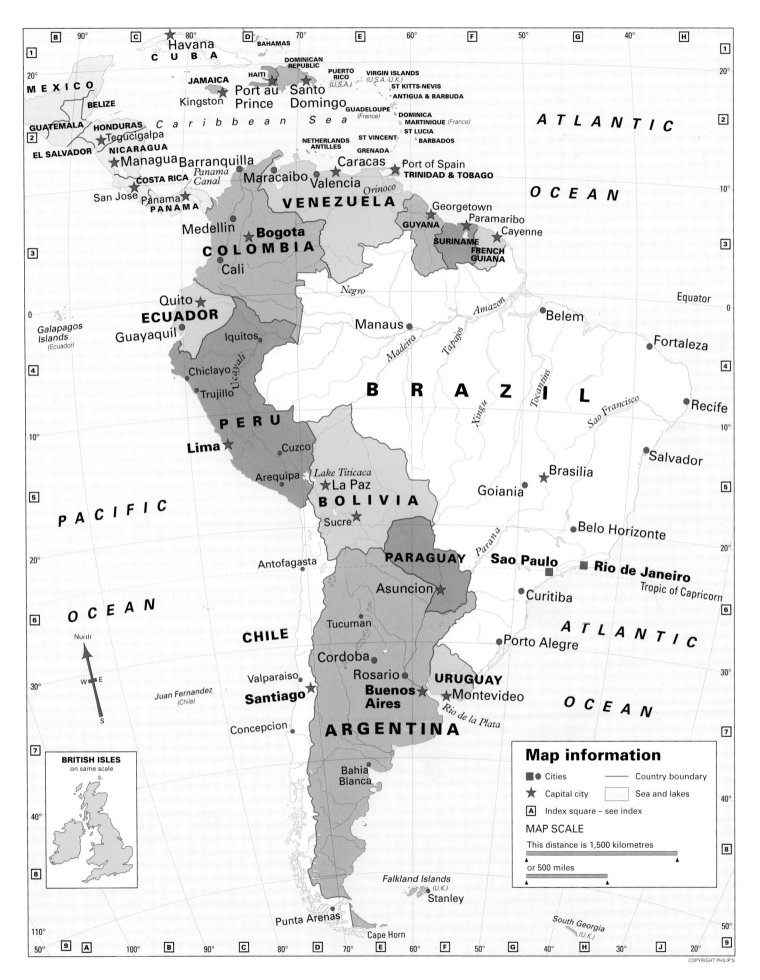

Havana
C U B A
BAHAMAS

MEXICO
BELIZE

GUATEMALA
HONDURAS
Tegucigalpa
EL SALVADOR
NICARAGUA
Managua
COSTA RICA
San Jose
Panama
Canal
PANAMA

JAMAICA
Kingston
HAITI
Port au
Prince
DOMINICAN
REPUBLIC
Santo
Domingo
PUERTO
RICO
(U.S.A.)
GUADELOUPE
(France)

VIRGIN ISLANDS
(U.S.A.-U.K.)
ST KITTS-NEVIS
ANTIGUA & BARBUDA
DOMINICA
MARTINIQUE (France)
ST LUCIA
BARBADOS
ST VINCENT
GRENADA
NETHERLANDS
ANTILLES

ATLANTIC

OCEAN

C a r i b b e a n   S e a

Barranquilla
Maracaibo
Valencia
Caracas
Port of Spain
TRINIDAD & TOBAGO

VENEZUELA

Medellin
Bogota
COLOMBIA
Cali

Orinoco

GUYANA
Georgetown
Paramaribo
Cayenne
SURINAME
FRENCH
GUIANA

Quito
ECUADOR
Guayaquil

Galapagos
Islands
(Ecuador)

Negro

Amazon
Equator

Manaus
Belem
Fortaleza

Iquitos

Chiclayo
Trujillo

Ucayali
Madeira
Tapajos
Xingu
Tocantins

B R A Z I L

Sao Francisco

Recife

PERU

Lima
Cuzco
Arequipa
Lake Titicaca
La Paz
BOLIVIA
Sucre

Salvador

Brasilia
Goiania

Belo Horizonte

PACIFIC

Antofagasta

PARAGUAY
Asuncion

Parana
Sao Paulo
Rio de Janeiro
Tropic of Capricorn
Curitiba

ATLANTIC

CHILE
Tucuman

Valparaiso
Santiago
Cordoba
Rosario
**Buenos
Aires**
URUGUAY
Montevideo
Rio de la Plata

OCEAN

Porto Alegre

OCEAN

Juan Fernandez
(Chile)

Concepcion

ARGENTINA

North
W   E
S

Bahia
Blanca

Falkland Islands
(U.K.)
Stanley

Punta Arenas
Cape Horn

South Georgia
(U.K.)

Map information

■ ● Cities   —— Country boundary
★ Capital city   ▢ Sea and lakes
Ⓐ Index square – see index

MAP SCALE

This distance is 1,500 kilometres

or 500 miles

COPYRIGHT PHILIP'S

61

Polar Regions

The Polar Regions are the areas around the North Pole and the South Pole. The area around the North Pole is called the **Arctic** and the area around the South Pole is called the **Antarctic**. The sun never shines straight down on the Arctic or Antarctic so they are very cold – the coldest places on Earth. The Arctic consists of frozen water. Some parts of Northern Europe, North America and Asia are inside the Arctic Circle. A group of people called the Inuit live there.

Map information

- Cities and towns

★ Capital cities

○ (Japan) Scientific stations in the Antarctic

Land covered in ice

Sea covered in ice

Ice sometimes in the sea

MAP SCALE
This distance is
1,500 kilometres

or 500 miles

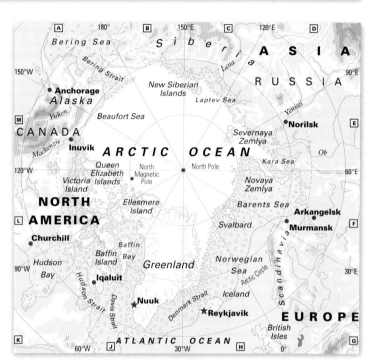

The Antarctic is a continent. It is bigger than Europe or Australia and has no permanent population. Most of the land consists of ice which is thousands of metres thick. At the edges, chunks of ice break off to make icebergs. These float out to sea. The diagram below shows a cross-section through Antarctica between two of the scientific research stations, Siple and Casey. It shows how thick the ice is on the ice sheets.

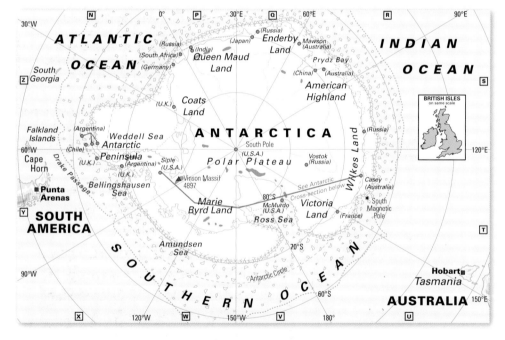

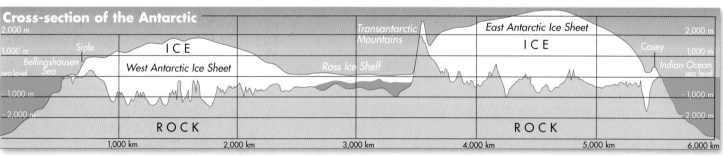

UK, Europe and the World

United Nations

The UN is the largest international organization in the world. The headquarters are in New York and 192 countries are members. It was formed in 1945 to help solve world problems and to help keep world peace. The UN sends peacekeeping forces to areas where there are problems.

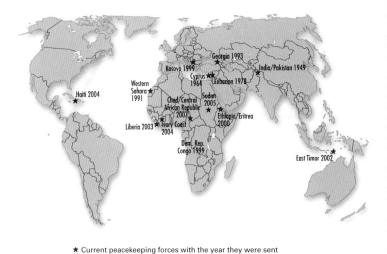

★ Current peacekeeping forces with the year they were sent

European Union

Population (million people)	
Austria	8
Belgium	10
Bulgaria	7
Cyprus	0.8
Czech Republic	10
Denmark	5
Estonia	1
Finland	5
France	61
Germany	82
Greece	11
Hungary	10
Ireland	4
Italy	58
Latvia	2
Lithuania	4
Luxembourg	0.5
Malta	0.4
Netherlands	16
Poland	39
Portugal	11
Romania	22
Slovak Republic	5
Slovenia	2
Spain	40
Sweden	9
UK	61

EU member countries

The EU was first formed in 1951. Six countries were members. Now there are 27 countries in the EU. These countries meet to discuss agriculture, industry and trade as well as social and political issues. The headquarters are in Brussels. Cyprus, the Czech Republic, Estonia, Hungary, Latvia, Lithuania, Malta, Poland, the Slovak Republic and Slovenia joined the EU in 2004. Bulgaria and Romania joined in 2007.

The Commonwealth

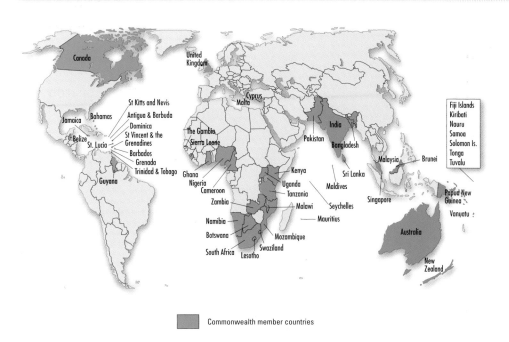

Commonwealth member countries

The Commonwealth is a group of 53 independent countries which used to belong to the British Empire. It is organized by a group of people called the Secretariat which is based in London. Queen Elizabeth II is the head of the Commonwealth. About every two years the heads of the different governments meet to discuss world problems. These meetings are held in different countries in the Commonwealth.

Index

The names in the index are in alphabetical order. To find a place on a map in the atlas, first find the name in the index. The first number after the place name is the page number. After the page number there is a letter and another number. The **letter** shows you the **column** where the place is on the map and the **number** shows you the **row**. If the place name goes across more than one square, the reference is to the square where the name begins.

64